BORIS

By Jaap ter Haar

Illustrated By
Rien Poortvliet

TRANSLATED FROM THE DUTCH BY
Martha Mearns

ILLUSTRATED BY
Rien Poortvliet

BORIS

By Jaap ter Haar

Illustrated By
Rien Poortvliet

HARCOURT BRACE & COMPANY

Orlando   Atlanta   Austin   Boston   San Francisco   Chicago   Dallas   New York
Toronto   London

This edition is published by special
arrangement with Delacorte Press/Seymour
Lawrence, a division of Bantam Doubleday
Dell Publishing Group, Inc.

Grateful acknowledgment is made to
Delacorte Press/Seymour Lawrence, a
division of Bantam Doubleday Dell
Publishing Group, Inc. for permission to
reprint *Boris* by Jaap ter Haar, illustrated by
Rien Poortvliet. Copyright © 1966 by Van
Dishoeck, Van Holkema and Warendorf N.V.,
Bussum; English translation copyright
© 1969 by Blackie & Son Limited.

Printed in the United States of America

ISBN 0-15-302232-9

4 5 6 7 8 9 10   011   97 96 95 94

BORIS

By Jaap ter Haar

Illustrated By
Rien Poortvliet

1

Boris Makarenko lay asleep. In the distance the German guns roared. High explosives, incendiaries and shells bombarded dying Leningrad, the city that was too proud and too courageous to surrender. It was December 1942.

Boris Makarenko slept and dreamed. Nearly always it was the same dream . . .

Cautiously the long line of lorries zig-zagged its way over frozen Lake Ladoga. Where were the safe places . . . ? Where were the cracks . . . ? It seemed that death rode with the convoy, hovering over the trucks as they laboured with food and supplies towards besieged, starving Leningrad.

Skidding wheels . . . cracking ice . . . spattering water. In the dark depths on the left Zolymski and his co-driver were slowly drowning. Their heavy lorry had got out of control as the ice cracked under the wheels. The bonnet had slipped between the icefloes. Slowly, very slowly, a precious crate of food disappeared into the icy water, then the lorry . . . The convoy travelled on. No one could stop to help. They had their orders.

In the distance the German guns roared . . . the first light of early morning began to show on the horizon . . . the freezing night was nearly over.

In his dream Boris was sitting beside his father. 'To the

left,' he murmured in his sleep. 'Father, drive to the left, to the left . . . !' He wanted to shout the words aloud but his voice would not come. In his dream he could see the set, calm face of his father through a kind of mist. His father peered through the frozen windscreen at the ice, at the track of the lorries twisting through the snow. He turned the steering, not to the left but to the *right* . . .

Suddenly a black speck appeared in the cloudy sky. There was a horrible roar and a single fighter plane dived down. Machine-guns began to rattle. The ice shattered into stars and the water foamed as the first bombs exploded. Father tried to stop a skid and turned the wheel further to the right. Behind their lorry lurched Ivanov's. The ice broke . . . Next came Pavlitchko with a cracked windscreen. His lorry disappeared through the hole in the ice. Lorry, men and food were lost in the depths of the lake . . .

Sobbing in his sleep, Boris turned his head here and there on the pillow, trying to escape from the dream. He muttered to himself and gripped the blankets with both hands . . .

Like maddened elephants now the lorries swerved crazily over the ice trying to avoid the bullets and shells.

With skidding wheels his father's lorry reeled over

the white flatness. Did he see that huge dark patch where the ice had begun to melt?

'To the left! Drive to the left!'

But again his father made for the right. The distance to the dark patch got less and less. Now it was only forty yards away, now thirty, now twenty. There was a ridge on the ice, a last frail wall of snow. It was only a few yards away. The crashing of ice was even louder than the roar of the engine. The front wheels skidded through the layer of snow. The lorry stopped for a moment, then the back wheels went. With a crash the load of boxes and sacks of supplies fell among the breaking ice. Dark water covered the snow. The engine spluttered . . .

Slowly, very slowly, the lorry sank between the ice-floes into the icy cold water. Deeper and still deeper . . .

Boris woke with a start. Again he had been dreaming about the convoy in which his father had lost his life. It was so vivid that he could not believe it was only a dream.

What happened daily in besieged Leningrad was like a thousand nightmares at once. The German soldiers surrounded the city. They were determined either to starve out the people or flatten the city – every day more than three hundred bombs and shells were hurled at it. Boris might well have dreamed of the hundreds of people who each week died in the streets of hunger and exhaustion; of the soldiers who time and again crawled back wounded from the fighting lines around the city; of the streets and houses that collapsed in flames; of the women who went crying among the ruins as they looked in vain for their children.

Leningrad indeed seemed a dying city. There was no

longer any running water, gas or electricity, or any public transport. The whole city was disrupted. For the most part people showed astounding patience and courage, though some behaved like animals, forgetting all decency in the terrible struggle for life.

Boris could have dreamed about the overwhelming hunger, about the women and children who stood in queues in more than twenty degrees of frost to get a jug of watery soup or a piece of bread. In hundreds of houses lay the dying and the dead, but all fear and sorrow were forgotten in the daily business of living. Suffering was inevitable in war – it had to be lived through, because life just had to go on.

The lorries of Boris's dream seemed much more real to him than what was happening around him, simply because his father had been a driver in the convoy. When the wide lake of Ladoga froze, lorries with essential medical supplies, food and ammunitions could travel across it. People could then manage to slip through the German lines and so relieve at least a part of the abominable want in Leningrad. In his imagination, Boris had driven with his father dozens of times. He knew only too well how the men sat in the driving-cabins and how the heavy trucks inched their way over the white, treacherous ice. He knew how the drivers were tormented by fear, and how unlimited was their courage. At the beginning of winter when the ice was still not very thick, and in the spring when it was beginning to thaw, the worry for his father's safety had been almost unbearable. At these times the water would seep over the wheels of the loaded trucks. On every expedition almost half of one convoy never came back at all. But still the survivors set out again the following day. Each lorry that managed to make the journey would save the lives of many people; each lorry that was lured by death into the lake took with it the lives of an unknown number of men, women and children in the city.

Boris often had nightmares about the lorries. Each time his father's lorry veered in the wrong direction, then disappeared into the depths – and Boris would wake up, clammy with sweat, for minutes afterwards still held in the grip of the terrible dream. Its horror would sometimes haunt him through the day . . .

His mother's bed creaked. She raised herself up on her pillow.

'Boris, are you awake?'

Boris opened his eyes. In the faint early light he saw the familiar room: the planks that his father had nailed over the window after the panes had been shattered during an air-raid, the stove in the corner where there was now no fire burning, his mother's bed, the lamp hanging crookedly from the ceiling, the cracks in the walls . . .

Boris flung off the blankets. It was icy cold in the room. As quickly as he could he pulled on his clothes and thrust his feet into his shoes. Then he went over to his mother's bed.

'You had better go to the canteen right away.'

Boris nodded. In the distance the guns still roared. He looked at his mother. He decided not to ask her how she felt. She would only answer that she felt much better and that she had had a good night's sleep, as if he were still a child that didn't know better. In her feverish eyes Boris could see anxiety and fear as well as illness. His mother was smiling at him, trying to pretend that she was quite well. Boris smiled in return. He too pretended all was well, just because he was no longer a child. Anyone who was twelve years old and had survived almost two years of the siege was certainly quite grown up.

'Wrap up well.'

Boris nodded again. He looked at his mother's suffering face. There were little sores caused by lack of food on her right cheek and along her upper lip. Her gentle brown eyes were hazy and in them he seemed to see a shadow. Was his mother going to die . . . ?

'Shall I go and ask Dr. Kirov to come?' Boris asked this question from time to time, but his mother always shook her head. The doctor would not have any time. He must give all his attention to the soldiers who came wounded from the front lines and to the people hurt in the air-raids. Against hunger and exhaustion Dr. Kirov could not begin to fight, however much he wanted to. Hundreds of people died in the city every day. That was part of the price that Leningrad had to pay to keep her freedom.

'There's something else that I want you to do for me,' said his mother. With a hint of a smile she put out her hand and pulled Boris towards her. 'You must go and see Uncle Vanya. Ask him if he will put your name on the list of children who are to be evacuated.'

Now there was no doubt at all in Boris's mind that he could see death lurking in her eyes.

'Boris, dear, it would be much better for you to get away from the city.'

'No!' said Boris. 'Never!' He knew that the lorries that travelled over Lake Ladoga with supplies sometimes took women and children back with them. But not for the most wonderful food parcel in the world would Boris travel in a lorry over that terrible water . . . over the dreadful weak patches of ice where his father had drowned. Not

14

for the world would he drive over the frozen waters of the
lake. And apart from his own terror, it was unthinkable
that he should forsake his mother and leave her to die
alone.

'The war might last for years yet,' said his mother. She
tried to get up, and looked imploringly at Boris. 'I want
you to go. You must go!'

'And what will you do without me?'

'I shall be all right.'

'Who will bring you food and water then?'

'By the time you go away I shall be quite well again.'

There was no point in arguing. Whatever happened, he would not go. To bring an end to the conversation Boris leaned over and kissed his mother on the forehead.

They looked at each other earnestly, both thinking their own thoughts. Boris: 'Is she going to die? Does she want to get me out of the way so that she can die alone? Does she want to spare me the pain of seeing her die?' His mother: 'Let him leave here. Oh God, don't let him stay in this city. Let him live!' Boris was all that she had now. She hadn't the strength to keep on living for his sake but she was determined that he would not die for hers.

Boris straightened his shoulders. 'I'll go and see if there is any food.'

'Wrap up well,' said his mother again.

Boris put on his scarf and his fur cap. It was still quite dark. He took the lamp from the table and shone it into the dresser to find a pan.

'Is there anything I can do for you?'

His mother shook her head.

Boris fastened his coat tightly. Hoping that his mother was not watching him, he slipped his father's old army revolver into his pocket. It was good to feel something belonging to his father close to him. It gave him a bit of extra courage.

From the door he waved to his mother as if he were setting out for school on any ordinary day. She mustn't see how troubled he was because that would make her more unhappy. With the pan under his arm Boris went down the crumbling steps . . .

2

The sounds of the city met Boris as he walked along the street: the pounding and scraping of picks and shovels as workers tried to clear heaps of rubble that had frozen fast in the snow; the marching footsteps of a company of soldiers; a radio-car calling for volunteers for some other salvage operation; the distant wailing of a siren. But Boris didn't hear these sounds. He was thinking of his mother who was perhaps going to die, and of the mothers of Peter, Serge, Ivan, Vladi and dozens of other children. They must get food. That was the first essential. Boris hoped very hard that this time he would manage to get a decent portion of soup at the canteen. The last time it had been much too small, but his protest hadn't done any good.

The icy wind blew along the streets. Boris clutched his pan closer and pulled his cap further down over his ears. On the other side of the street stood the ghostly shells of bombed-out houses, spectres in the snowy grey light. He noticed an old man lying near a heap of rubble. A thin layer of snow had covered him during the night. He was dead. Boris tried not to look at him and not to think about him. Very soon the big van would drive through the streets to take away his body and probably the bodies of hundreds of other people.

When the bombardment of Leningrad had begun, and he had first seen dead people lying in the streets, Boris had wept. Then his father had pulled him close to him and spoken to him earnestly: 'We must be brave, Boris. Every person in Leningrad must be brave. The courage that we will show will give courage to other people. And only with courage and still more courage shall we withstand the enemy.'

Father had wiped away Boris's tears and since then he had never cried again. Of course he had been afraid and sometimes he felt very sad. Sometimes he had been bewildered and horrified by the terrible things that he saw happening in the city. But he had never cried, not even when Zaretsky came to tell him that his father had died a hero's death for the sake of Russia and freedom. That had cost him the biggest effort of his whole life.

Boris walked on, still thinking of his mother. She must go on living. What was the use of freedom if she was going to die? He must see that she got something to eat. The watery beetroot soup that they got from the canteen was not enough, even if he gave some of his own ration to his mother without telling her. He wondered how many times his mother had done the same thing for him . . .

'Boris, wait for me!'

Boris looked round. It was Nadia running after him. She was wearing her brother's shoes and they were far too big for her. Her breath came white over the woollen scarf that she had wrapped round her neck up to her nose.

Boris was delighted to see her. Now he wouldn't have to walk all the rest of the long way to the canteen by himself. Nadia was two years older than he was so perhaps he could talk to her about his mother. He would have liked to have made a joke about the size of Nadia's shoes – they were like boats on her skinny feet – but when he looked at her closer, he kept quiet. Nadia's face was dead white and tense, as if something dreadful had happened. Tears rolled down her cheeks on to her woollen scarf. Was she really crying or were the tears caused by the cold icy wind?

Boris didn't ask her anything. Together they walked along the path dug out between the snow-covered ruins of the houses.

'I hope we get something really nice to eat today,' said Boris.

He tried hard to think of something that would cheer Nadia up but he couldn't think of anything.

'It will be beetroot soup again,' said Nadia. 'We won't get anything else for a few days yet, until the lake has frozen hard enough to bear the weight of the lorries.'

'Well, a few days is not very long,' said Boris. He peered at Nadia from under his furry cap. Her face was so forlorn.

'A few days will really go very quickly,' said Boris again.

'It had better freeze hard,' said Nadia. 'If there is a thaw, we shall have to wait much longer.'

They turned the corner and came to the square where the statues stood buried under piles of sand-bags. Then they walked along a narrow street where all the windows had been boarded up with thick planks of wood.

Again Boris looked at Nadia. She looked as sad or even sadder than before. This was certainly no time to make any jokes about her shoes. Boris had never seen Nadia look anything but happy before. She could always think of funny things to say or do and was always making people laugh. Something very dreadful must have happened – but he didn't like to ask her what it was. Boris fingered the revolver in his pocket, and he thought of what his father had said: 'The courage that we show will give courage to other people.' Could he say this to Nadia?

From a passing radio-car came the voice of an announcer

giving the latest news of the war. The fight against the Germans was going on in many other places in Russia. Were these people also getting beetroot soup to eat? With a stab of regret, Boris thought of all the food he had refused to eat before the war, just because he didn't like the taste or the look of it. If only he had the chance of it now. His mouth began to water. If only he could have some of that food now to give to his mother.

'When I'm grown up, I'm going to be a soldier,' he said to Nadia. It was better not to think about eating because that made you twice as hungry.

'When you are grown-up the war will be over,' said Nadia. A little smile appeared on her strained face.

'I hope not,' muttered Boris. He wanted to fight the Germans who had killed his father; it was their fault that thousands of people were dying in Leningrad; that the cheerful houses were lying in ruins; that everyone was hungry.

'I want to be a doctor,' said Nadia.

'I thought you wanted to act in films,' said Boris.

Nadia shook her head, but said nothing. She seemed to be lost again in her own thoughts.

They walked past a big church. Two old women carrying a cross were struggling arm in arm up the icy steps in front of it. Were they going to pray to God to help Leningrad? Were they going to pray for peace?

'Do you believe in God, Nadia?' asked Boris.

'No,' said Nadia. She sounded so fierce that Boris still didn't dare to ask her what was wrong. His mother had always told him that God cared for everyone – but why did He not do something to bring an end to all this misery?

They came within sight of the canteen. The queue of waiting women and children was not as long as on some days. It would be their turn in an hour or so . . .

Slowly they moved forward. Nadia seemed very impatient. She kept looking nervously about her as if there was someone she was afraid of among the people who waited.

'What is it?' asked Boris.

'Sssh,' said Nadia angrily. She clutched her ration card tightly in her hand. It was almost their turn now, but she didn't move forward. In spite of the cold her face was still as white as death.

'Come on, next please,' called the man who was ladling out the soup.

Nadia still hesitated for a moment. She looked timidly at the canteen workers and she still didn't give up her ration card. Boris saw her hands were trembling.

'Has your card been marked?'

'Go on,' murmured Boris. He gave Nadia a little push. At last she took a step forward. She gave her card to a man, who stamped it, his hand raw and red with cold.

'Four portions,' called the man.

Boris leaned over to see how full they filled Nadia's pan. She got four brimming ladlefuls, and it looked as if the soup was thicker than usual that day. There seemed to be pieces of meat in it and bits of potato too. Was Nadia pleased with her big ration? Boris could not tell. With an expressionless face and cast-down eyes she went quickly out again. She held the pan close to her as if she was frightened that someone was going to take it from her.

Now it was Boris's turn. Anxiously he watched the ladle dip into the soup. A shiver of disappointment ran through him when it came out again. It was not quite full. Boris looked imploringly at the man but he was afraid to say anything. The second ladleful was a bit bigger . . . but it was not full to the brim.

Tears sprang into Boris's eyes.

'My mother is ill,' he whispered.

'Next one,' called the man with the rubber stamp, and the woman behind Boris pushed him aside. Slowly he went outside, where Nadia was standing waiting for him.

'Did you manage to get any extra?' asked Nadia. Boris shook his head. He could not trust himself to answer because of the lump in his throat. Then he looked at Nadia and was surprised to see that she was smiling at him. It was the first time that day he had seen her look happy.

'Bring your pan over here,' she ordered. She took off the lid of her pot and poured some of the soup into Boris's.

'But . . . but . . . Nadia,' said Boris in astonishment, 'what are you doing?'

'Be quiet,' said Nadia. She looked around to make sure nobody could hear her. 'You must tell no one,' she said quickly. 'You must not say a word. Don't even tell your mother that I have given you some of our food. If you do, something terrible might happen to us.'

'But why?' asked Boris, not understanding.

'Do you remember Stipolev?' whispered Nadia.

Boris nodded. Stipolev had been one of their neighbours. He had altered the marks in some ration cards and in a starving city that was the worst crime that anybody could commit. The fraud had been discovered, soldiers had come to arrest Stipolev, and he had been shot without further question.

'I've been cheating too,' whispered Nadia. Tears streamed down her white face. 'Boris, don't tell anyone. Please don't say a word to anyone.'

'But what have you done?' Boris looked at her anxiously. He just could not imagine that Nadia could do anything dishonest.

Nadia hung her head. 'My father died yesterday,' she murmured, 'and when I awoke this morning, Serjozja was dead too . . .' Serjozja was her brother.

Suddenly Boris understood. Now there were only Nadia and her mother, two people, but she had managed to get four portions.

'Oh, Nadia!' said Boris. He didn't even notice that he too was crying as they walked back along the streets.

3

For a long time they walked on in silence, both lost in their own thoughts. Then, when they came to the church, Nadia spoke again.

'I did it for my mother, Boris. I did it for her.'

Boris understood why she had done it, but still, it was not honest. There were hundreds of hungry mothers, hundreds of starving fathers, hundreds of children desperate for food. In Leningrad everyone was allotted the same rations. Whenever there was any food in the city it was divided out as fairly as possible – there was no question about that.

Boris sneaked another look at Nadia. She wasn't crying any more, but her guilty conscience showed clearly on her face. Her crime was so tiny but so terrible . . .

Boris simply did not know what he should say to her. Her father had died. Serjozja, too, would never waken again. He wondered if their bodies were still lying in the room where Nadia and her mother had to sleep – or had the big van already taken them away?

'I'll give you some more of my soup,' said Nadia softly.

They walked on slowly, side by side, across the square with its statues. Boris shook his head; he was ashamed of himself . . . Just that morning, as he had stood beside his mother's bed, he had prayed for a miracle to happen. Was Nadia's meddling with the ration cards the miracle for which he had hoped?

But what if anyone found out? Would they shoot Nadia for her crime? Boris shuddered. Perhaps it would be better if they went together and confessed it all.

'Are you coming?' asked Nadia. They began to walk through a small park. Nadia stopped at a place where the bushes hid them from passers-by.

'Take the lid off your soup-pan!'

Boris hesitated and then did as he was told. Careful not to spill a drop, Nadia poured more of her soup into it. Boris didn't protest. Now he was an accomplice; that he understood only too well. But he, too, did it for his mother.

'Promise you won't say a word to anyone,' whispered Nadia.

'I promise,' whispered Boris.

Nadia smiled. Her face looked less strained as they walked back through the park towards the square.

'Watch you don't spill your soup,' called one of the soldiers on guard beside an anti-aircraft gun. All the men were stamping their feet and slapping their arms together, trying to keep warm.

Boris nodded, more to himself than to the soldiers. Of course he would watch that he didn't spill any of his own or the extra ration which he had no right to have. It was such a pleasant feeling, in spite of his guilt, to know that in a little while he would be able to give his mother a great big helping. Her bowl would be nearly full, and it was such a lovely thick soup today!

He smiled at Nadia. How sad she looked as she thought of her father and brother! Perhaps it was a comfort to her that he was involved in her crime now and could share her guilt.

They came to the gate of the park, where they had to wait. A convoy of lorries filled with soldiers was rolling past slowly. The soldiers were packed into the trucks. They had rifles on their shoulders. As they passed they laughed and waved to Boris and Nadia. Boris was sorry he could not wave back, but he had to hold on to his pan with both hands. Were they going to the front to fight against the Germans? Later on he would be among them. Later, when he was old enough, he would fight alongside them to free Leningrad.

Suddenly – right behind them – a siren screamed. Boris jumped with fright. His pan bumped against Nadia's side and some of the soup spilled on the ground. In silent rage Boris looked at the pieces of beetroot lying in the snow. From all parts of the city now the sirens gave out their warning.

'This way,' said Nadia. On the corner of the square was a notice saying where the nearest shelter was. People were running across the square in all directions. The soldiers in the anti-aircraft artillery unit frantically got their guns in position.

Nadia began to run and Boris jogged after her. But with each step the soup slopped against the lid. It kept on spilling.

'Not so fast,' he called after Nadia.

The convoy of lorries did not stop. The last lorry in the line was now passing them.

'Don't be afraid! We'll get them this time,' shouted a young soldier, with his helmet tipped carelessly over one ear. Boris was not afraid. After all, the sirens had sounded in Leningrad hundreds of times before. The only thing he was afraid of was that he might lose another drop of soup.

'It will be all right,' said Nadia. She seemed to be try- ing to hold her breath as if that would somehow stop her spilling even a drop of her soup. As quickly as they could manage it, they scuttled over the street towards the shelter.

Then a hundred things seemed to happen at once. First Boris heard a high-pitched drone coming at them from the side. In a flash he saw a German plane diving towards them through the clouds. An old woman was struggling across the square from the other side. A mother with two children was desperately looking for a place to shelter.

'Quickly, quickly,' shouted Nadia, her voice breaking.

They ran back towards the park. Machine-guns began to rattle. Everywhere people rushed this way and that looking for a place to hide. Some threw themselves flat on the street.

'Quicker, Boris,' sobbed Nadia. But Boris was still concentrating on his soup. He pressed down the lid with his thumb while he ran awkwardly after Nadia.

The sound of the aeroplane's engine was deafening now. It was directly overhead. Nadia swerved to the left and tried to shelter behind the low wall of the park. There was an ear-splitting explosion. Boris felt himself lifted up. Then he was thrown to the pavement with the blast.

'My soup,' thought Boris, half-dazed, as he fell heavily on the hard ground. There was a deathly silence. It seemed as if the whole world was breathlessly waiting. Stiff with fright, Boris lay in the snow with his eyes tightly shut.

Then slowly the sound of the aeroplane faded in the direction of Neva. As if in a dream, Boris heard running footsteps. Orders were rapped out and then someone in the square shouted for help.

'Rotters, hooligans, murderers . . . !' A man shook his fists at the sky in helpless rage . . . There was the sound of a woman crying and groans from those who had been wounded . . .

28

The running footsteps came nearer. Boris was aware of someone bending over him.

'Are you all right?' said a voice.

Slowly Boris opened his eyes. A soldier from the anti-aircraft division was leaning over him.

'Do you feel any pain? Are you wounded?'

Still dazed with shock, Boris shook his head. Then he saw Nadia clambering to her feet a few yards away. She had a big black mark on her face where her head had hit the ground. Her stockings were all torn. She brushed the snow and sand off her coat. She looked as if she was walking in her sleep.

'Boris, Boris . . . Oh, Boris!' she murmured. She suddenly looked very small and helpless standing there in the snow. She just stood and stared at the ground.

Then Boris understood what she was looking at. Her pan, overturned, lay there in the snow. The soup had spilled all over the ground. Pieces of beetroot, scraps of meat and lumps of potato lay there wasted.

Again Boris looked at the soldier and then at his own pan. It lay empty where it had fallen, its contents also scattered in the snow. He pulled off his mittens and tried to pick up some of the pieces of food.

'Let it be, lad,' said the soldier gently. But Boris crouched sorrowfully in the snow. He didn't look up because he didn't want the soldier to see that he was crying.

Nadia came and sat beside him. Without saying a word, she put her arm round his shoulder.

In spite of all the terrible confusion, the soldier paused and looked at the children. He saw the precious soup seeping into the snow. It was a tragedy, but a small one. Because he was a soldier he could not let routine be upset by such a trivial event . . . soldiers had seen much greater tragedies in starving Leningrad.

'Too bad, kids,' he said, 'but a lot worse things have happened in the world.' Then he strode off towards the square where the people who had been hurt were still crying for help.

'Come on, Boris,' said Nadia. She picked up the pans, helped Boris to his feet, and pushed him in the direction away from the square. She thought they would go home the long way round. It was bad enough to know what was happening in the square without having to see it.

They were both still suffering from shock as they walked through the park carrying their empty pans. They were both wondering if this was a punishment for having been dishonest at the canteen. But if it was their punishment, why had all the people in the square and the convoy of soldiers been bombed too?

Boris felt dull and empty as he dragged himself along. What was he to say to comfort his mother when he came back empty-handed?

'Never mind, Boris,' said Nadia. 'I know another way to get some food.'

Her words were so unexpected and so unbelievable that Boris stood still.

'I'll tell you in a minute,' said Nadia, because she was not quite sure if Boris would be willing to take part in her dangerous plan.

Coming down the street towards them was a group of salvage workers, both men and women. They were on their way to the place where the bomb had fallen.

4

'Now, listen,' said Nadia, when they had passed the salvage workers.

Boris's heart beat faster. He knew from the way that Nadia looked at him – intently and yet mysteriously – that he was going to hear some terrible secret.

'I know where there are lots of potatoes,' said Nadia. Her eyes shone with triumph.

Boris stared at her in absolute astonishment. The only potatoes that were to be found in Leningrad were stored in sacks at the canteen. After what had happened that morning, surely Nadia couldn't have taken it into her head to make a raid on the stores? For a moment he was speechless, then he asked doubtfully: 'Where are these potatoes of yours, then?'

Nadia took a deep breath. She wondered, even then, if it was wise to take Boris into her confidence. Then she made up her mind.

'They're in a field outside the city, in pits in the ground.' The words were out. She watched for Boris's reaction.

'Oh, those potatoes,' mumbled Boris in disappointment. The fields outside the city were out of reach, for they lay in No-man's-land, the territory between the German and Russian lines. It was forbidden to go there, and anyone who disobeyed would be in peril of his life. Boris felt completely let down. What was the use of knowing where there were potatoes if you could not get at them? Why on earth had Nadia raised his hopes so pointlessly?

'But I know how to get there,' said Nadia quickly. She moved closer to Boris and gripped his arm. 'Serjozja told me yesterday before we went to sleep.' She whispered the words, trying to make him realize how important they were.

Boris looked at her, shamefaced. His brief doubts about Nadia vanished and he felt sorry that he had lacked faith in her, even for a moment. Serjozja had said it. Surely that altered everything. He understood now why Nadia was determined to put her dangerous plan into action. Serjozja had told her before he had gone to sleep, never to waken again . . . Boris was convinced that no one so near death would have wicked thoughts and surely everyone's last words should be taken seriously.

'Isn't it very difficult to get into No-man's-land?'

Nadia shook her head. 'I know exactly the way we can go there,' she said with great assurance. 'I know exactly how!'

Boris nodded. In a way it was marvellous to think about this plan, to be able to forget for a while about all the other horrible things that were happening.

The long slow wail of the sirens gave the signal that the alarm was over. From everywhere people began to appear. An old woman got painfully to her feet and picked up the two cans of water that she had been carrying before the raid. Life began again . . . Full of their plan, Nadia and Boris walked past the ghostly, forsaken houses towards their own street.

'You must bring a sack with you and a small spade if you can. Something that you can hide under your coat,' said Nadia.

Boris nodded again. He would bring the coal-shovel. After all it had been lying useless for ages in the empty coal-cellar.

'And don't forget to tell your mother that you will be out for a long time.' This was good advice, but Boris had already begun to wonder to himself what excuse he would be able to make, to keep his mother from worrying about him.

When they arrived at Nadia's house they agreed that they would go on this dangerous expedition as soon as possible. Boris stared fixedly at the ground. He didn't dare look up at the windows on the first floor where Nadia lived. Stealthily Boris glanced across the street from under his fur cap. He was relieved to see that the old man who had been lying there that morning had gone, but he could still see quite clearly the shape his body had made in the snow . . .

Boris had always found it very difficult not to tell his mother the truth. Now he decided that he would say that the food hadn't been given out at the canteen because of the air-raid and that he had to go back in the afternoon. With his back to his mother's bed he muttered that he was going somewhere else with Nadia – a sort of half-truth which sounded to him like a real, enormous lie.

'Promise me that you will go and talk to Uncle Vanya!'

With a jerk Boris turned round. So his mother was absolutely serious about sending him away from the city.

'No,' he said stubbornly. 'I won't go. Whatever happens I am going to stay with you.'

His mother's hands twitched the sheets nervously, as if she were trying to get some sort of support from them. Then she looked at Boris so long and so searchingly that he could not meet her eyes. But surely she could see for herself that he was no longer a child.

'Boris, hand me the writing-paper and a pen.'

So she hadn't seen anything different about him. Boris realized that she was about to write a letter to the evacuation committee, but he didn't protest. There were probably dozens of mothers writing heart-breaking letters to the committee. When he came home again with his potatoes, she would at least realize how necessary he was to her. That evening, when he had really accomplished something, his mother would be convinced that he wasn't a child any longer, and admit that he need not be sent away with the others.

Quickly he picked up the paper, the ink-bottle and the pen. He put them on the little cabinet beside her bed. Then he filled her glass with water from the big jug in the corner. Before his mother had the chance to look at him again, because she was sure to see something suspicious in his face, he kissed her lightly on her cheek.

'Good-bye, Mother.' The words sounded just as he had meant them to, light-hearted and cheerful, as if he were merely going out to play.

He found the coal-shovel in the cellar and stuck it in the belt of his trousers. Next he stuffed an old sack, which he also found in the cellar, under his coat. Feeling conspicuously bulky, he went out into the street. The old service revolver sat comfortingly in his pocket. He felt it against him, and it was as if his father were telling him that he was doing this for his mother's own good . . .

Nadia was waiting for him in the street. It seemed to Boris that she looked at him more earnestly than ever; she certainly inspected him from head to foot as he came up to her. Was she wondering if he was big enough to come? Did she doubt that he was brave enough?

Boris pulled back his shoulders and tried to make himself look taller.

'Well! Let's go,' he said abruptly.

Nadia smiled at him, and it was a warm, friendly smile. Obviously he had passed the test.

'Come on, then,' she said, taking Boris's hand. They walked through the streets: past the house where Stipolev lived, who had been shot because he had meddled with the ration cards; past Valentina Kalma's house – she had died like a hero in the front line; past Victor Zorov's house – he was now a prisoner-of-war in a far-distant camp; past Ivan and Nina's house, which was now nothing more than a burnt-out shell.

Nadia gave Boris's hand a firm little squeeze, as if to give him courage and show her confidence that everything was going to be all right.

Boris nodded to her, so that she would know that he wasn't afraid. Hadn't it been Serjozja who had thought up this plan?

Lorries loaded with debris, huge water-tanks, an ambulance, and trucks filled with soldiers drove through the streets. In some places there were queues of women and children waiting for water – a common sight since the main-pipe had frozen up. You could not get water from the taps, as Boris knew only too well; sometimes it was a terrible job to break the ice in the buckets because the houses were so cold now. Boris and Nadia said little, just from time to time a word or two about what they were going to do.

'I only hope there isn't another air-raid,' said Nadia, frowning.

Boris nodded again. An air-raid would certainly upset their plans.

'I hope the ice under the bridge will hold,' murmured Nadia a little later.

Boris fervently hoped so too.

'We've got a long, long way to go,' whispered Nadia one street further on.

Because she said so little Boris realized that Nadia was still very worried about the difficulties that were ahead of them. It was not going to be an easy journey. He walked on firmly beside her. They were going to do something that no one would approve of – he realized that. But somehow they must get food . . .

They passed a group of children who were playing at making war. They had built a shelter among the ruins of a bombed house. Their excited voices echoed down the street.

'You're the Germans and we're the Russians!'

'No, we want to be the Russians!' They had started to quarrel even before their war had begun – no one wanted to be a German.

They walked past a few shops which were still open; in front of them long queues of patiently waiting people had formed. They walked past notice-boards which urged the people of Leningrad to have courage, or gave them warning of where unexploded bombs lay.

Just as they reached the outskirts of the city, a soldier hailed them.

'Hey, you!'

Boris's heart jumped. Nadia, too, looked frightened. She let go of Boris's hand and clasped her arms against her chest as if she were desperately trying to protect a great secret.

'Do you know Barov Street?'

Boris looked helplessly at Nadia. He had never heard of Barov Street and Nadia didn't know either. Would the soldier send them back again if he discovered that they didn't belong to this district?

Nadia swallowed hard. Then she looked the soldier straight in the eyes. 'You must go along that street over there,' she said. 'Go left after two blocks and then ask someone else.'

'Thanks,' said the soldier, and to Boris's horror he patted him on the shoulder. Then he strode quickly in the direction Nadia had told him.

'Come on!' Nadia's voice sounded hard and she looked very grim. Boris didn't understand why she was pulling him on so quickly but he didn't say anything. He noticed that she kept looking back over her shoulder.

'I don't know where Barov Street is,' said Nadia after a while. 'But I had to say something.'

So that was it. And Nadia was feeling wretched because she quite probably sent the soldier in the wrong direction, a soldier who was fighting to keep them free. Now it was Boris's hand that gripped Nadia's more firmly to show her that he understood how she felt. A glimmer of a smile appeared on her face.

'I am so glad you came with me,' she said.

'So am I,' replied Boris. On the way he had been trying to decide how many potatoes they could manage to carry between them. With a bit of luck he and his mother would be able to live on potatoes for a month.

Now they had come to the end of the city streets. Barbed wire . . . tanks . . . women filling up craters with sand and rubble and building reinforcements . . . All the houses here were mere walls, blackened and empty, muti-

38

lated by bombs and shells. What had become of the people who had lived in them?

Boris and Nadia clambered over the ruins. At the end of the street they could see the look-out post standing out against the sky.

They were passing the very last houses now; bricks, girders and glass lay heaped up in what had been gardens. Everything here had been destroyed in the fighting.

'That's the way we have to go,' whispered Nadia, pointing over a stretch of debris, sand-bags and trenches, half-covered with a thin layer of snow. On a badly damaged signpost was the half-obliterated name of Novgorod, and in the distance Boris could see the Russian lines.

As quickly and as silently as they could, they dodged through the ruins. They came to more barbed wire. Boris felt his heart beating painfully. Nadia was now almost crawling on her hands and knees. He realized that from now on they must be seen by no one . . .

'Don't make a sound from now on,' whispered Nadia.

They were crouched in a shell-hole close to the bank of a stream that lay frozen in the gully between two high embankments. A hundred yards farther on were the Russian lines. There the soldiers kept guard over the heavy artillery, the ammunition and the machine-guns. Nadia watched their movements carefully; she looked around on all sides; then she touched Boris on the shoulder.

'Now!'

They clambered out of the hole, tried to make themselves as small as possible, and ran the last part to the river. They slid and skidded breathlessly down its steep bank. Now at last they were out of sight of the soldiers. And now also Boris could see how they could get back beyond the lines unobserved. They had only to walk along the river-bed. The one dangerous bit would be the bridge. Would Serjozja have paused there and wondered about it too?

Nadia was standing still, listening intently to all sounds. She was out of breath, and little puffs of white came from her lips. They could hear quite clearly the voices and laughs of the Russian soldiers.

'Come on.'

Without making a sound they crept through the stiff-frozen reeds towards the bridge. In the distance they heard a few scattered shots and the sound of a car starting.

Crack! The ice snapped under Boris's right foot. Nadia turned on him indignantly.

'Ssssssssh!'

Boris made a face at her. How could he help it if the ice was thin?

Almost on all fours they made their way through the reeds to the bridge. Now they would have to forsake the bank and entrust themselves to the ice. To his horror, Boris saw that the water in the middle under the bridge was not frozen. Dark, cold and threatening, it rippled in the icy wind. Would the few feet of ice that had formed against the concrete sides of the bridge be strong enough to hold them? Boris felt terror creeping over him; under the bridge was just like his nightmare: ice and black holes.

Even Nadia hesitated. Then she stepped cautiously on to the ice. It held. Slowly she shuffled – foot after foot, in Serjozja's huge comical boots – on to the narrow strip of ice under the bridge. Once there she turned and waved for him to follow.

Boris glanced about himself in panic. Scenes from his nightmare flashed before his eyes: the snow-covered plain that was Lake Ladoga; the splintering ice; his father's hand gripping the steering-wheel . . .

For a moment or two he stood trembling, struggling against fear. Then suddenly he could almost hear his father talking to him, as he had before his last fatal ride.

'It's not a sin to be afraid, Boris, for we can be brave at the same time.'

'Pssst!' Nadia was making frantic signs for him to hurry. Any second the soldiers might appear.

Boris took a deep breath. With a mighty effort, he tried

to think about his mother, about the potatoes, about Serjozja. Keeping his eyes turned away from the dark water, he stepped on to the strip of ice which seemed to grow narrower and narrower.

Nadia was half-way across. To make herself as light as possible she was supporting herself with her hands against the wall.

'It's a good job,' thought Boris ruefully, 'that we're both so skinny.' Inch by inch, he edged down until he too was under the bridge. The ice gave a creak and a crack shot through it. Black water began to seep through.

Boris moved forward as quickly as he dared; the sooner he was out of this dangerous spot the better. Then he realized Nadia was standing quite still. She raised her hand in warning. Boris heard for himself the marching footsteps of a detachment of troops. Their boots rang out on the bridge. Then a command: 'At the double!' The footsteps drummed on the bridge, just above their heads.

Boris stood like a stone. He shut his eyes in order not to see the ice and the water.

Nadia peered out and up anxiously; then she turned and almost giggled at Boris – as if they were sharing a joke at the expense of the soldiers. Boris tried to smile back at her, but it was a feeble effort. He'd better think of something nice quickly – how many potatoes he was going to carry home; his mother, who would almost cry with joy – but he wished with all his heart he were safe at home now.

It seemed an eternity before the soldiers' footsteps died away . . .

'Come!' Nadia beckoned.

Clinging to the underside of the bridge, Nadia and

Boris struggled painfully on. At last they were across the groaning, faintly heaving ice and on the other side of the bridge. Boris's heart lifted as he felt firm Russian soil beneath his feet once more – even if that soil was hard-frozen and hidden under a thick blanket of snow . . .

Boris gazed after Nadia – how incredibly brave she was! She had gone up the bank on the far side of the bridge, craning her neck and peering over to see if their way was clear. Boris felt ashamed that he had been such a coward. Cowards could never make fine soldiers. He resolved never again to be so unmanly.

Suddenly the sirens went off in Leningrad. From this distance they sounded much more ominous than when you were closer to them. Then Boris heard the monotonous drone of a group of bombers. Another attack from the air?

Nadia climbed back down hastily, her coat encrusted with snow.

'We're in luck,' she said excitedly. 'While there are planes overhead, no one will bother us.'

Boris nodded, although he was not too happy about this kind of luck. How many bombs would rain down on the city this time? The drone in the sky grew louder. In the distance the guns began again. Boris hoped they would hit their target – though it was a dreadful thought that the men in the air would crash-dive in flames to their deaths.

'Boom! Boom!' Almost deafening came the return shots from the German lines.

'Come on,' said Nadia, holding out her hand. As quickly as they could they ran along the bank. The distance between them and the bridge grew. They left behind

43

them the witch's cauldron of explosions and flames which was their city.

'We're in luck,' Nadia had said. Perhaps they really were in luck, since they had got so far from the city without being noticed. But Boris still heard the bombs dropping on Leningrad, where his mother lay helpless in bed.

Boris ran after Nadia. He tried not to think any longer. The only thing that mattered now were the pits of potatoes in the lonely waste of No-man's-land. Boris could see them now, covered with straw and sand. He saw himself digging and then . . . thousands of potatoes heaped together like marbles . . .

They sat in the snow. They had walked for more than an hour from the bridge. Leningrad and the Russian lines round the city lay far behind them among the gentle rolling countryside. On the way they had come upon a farm which had been burned to the ground. They had poked around it, but they hadn't found anything to eat. In the desolate yard had been an empty dog-kennel. What had happened to the dog, Boris wondered? Was it still alive? Or had the Germans shot it, as they sometimes shot people? Somehow, the dog-kennel made Boris sadder than the blackened ruins of the farm. After all, didn't he see blackened ruins every day? Without saying very much they had set off again. It was hard going on the frosty, uneven ground, against the cold wind. Boris's lips felt frost-bitten, and a place on the inside of his thigh was rubbed raw with the rough material of his trousers. They began to walk more and more slowly. Nadia, too, seemed suddenly to have become very tired.

'Let's have a rest,' she had said. And they had flopped down in the snow. They sucked pieces of snow to see if that would help their thirst, and perhaps also their gnawing hunger.

'Is it much farther?' Boris must have asked the same question at least ten times.

'It can't be much farther now,' said Nadia. She pointed to a row of trees in the distance. 'It must be over there.'

The trees looked a long way off, but now that the end was at least in sight, Boris began to feel a bit more cheerful. The way back wouldn't be so bad. They'd have the wind at their backs, and they'd also have the potatoes. With that precious loot the journey would be nothing. From under his fur cap Boris watched Nadia, who had kept going so steadily the whole way. Now she was gasping from exertion. Her breath came out of her mouth like puffs of smoke and was blown away by the wind.

'Nadia, have you ever been afraid?'

Nadia nodded.

'When?'

Nadia thought for a bit. 'When I'm at home,' she said at last. 'When I'm sitting in the room and feel that Father's got his eye on me . . .' Her voice trailed away. She had forgotten that her father and Serjozja were dead now. No wonder, with all the suspense of that afternoon.

It was deathly quiet in the white world around them. No sirens, no scraping of shovels, no guns. Shamefaced, because she had forgotten, Nadia gazed at the snow. She looked ready to burst into tears. Afterwards, when the war was over, he'd marry Nadia, Boris thought. Then he'd look after her, and she would never have to look so sad again. But what could he say to her now that would stop the trembling of her lips?

'I'm often afraid too!' he said softly.

'When I'm afraid I write my diary,' said Nadia.

'Does that help?'

'Sometimes.'

Boris stared into the distance. It might be an idea to keep a diary. You could write down things that you couldn't say aloud.

'We'd better go on,' said Nadia. They had got stiff, sitting in the cold. They shivered as they stood up.

Now it was Boris's turn to hold out his hand and help Nadia along. After the first few steps his trousers began to rub against the same sore place on his leg.

Hand in hand they plodded on through that still, white world. The trees stood out like slender, grey twigs against the horizon.

'It's not much farther,' said Boris cheerfully.

One foot after another. They *must* get there soon. But
it was slow going, so slow. Three-quarters of an hour
later they seemed to have covered hardly any ground.
The trees in the distance that Nadia had kept pointing to were still in the distance. Boris began to worry
again.

'Will we get back before it's dark?'

Nadia didn't answer. Perhaps she thought it was a
stupid question. Or was she too exhausted to speak? For
the last half-hour she hadn't said a single word, but just
stared silently ahead. Was she thinking about her father
and Serjozja?

One foot after another. At each step, Boris's worry
grew. How on earth were they going to manage to walk
back, if they had heavy bags of potatoes to carry? He decided not to look up from the ground until he had counted
a hundred. Perhaps after that, when he looked up, they
would be nearly at the trees. But no, when he had counted
as slowly as possible and looked up, the thin little twigs
still stood out against the sky. One foot after another.
Nadia tripped. She would have fallen if Boris hadn't
managed to hold her. He put his arm around her, but she
almost tripped again. Was it because Serjozja's boots
were far too big for her? She stopped and put her hand
to her head.

'Shall we have a rest?' Boris asked her.

Nadia didn't answer. Because the row of trees was still far away, Boris thought they had better carry on. But it was getting difficult to drag Nadia along now. Perhaps it would be better to sit down for a few minutes to gather their strength for the last bit. He was just going to say this, when Nadia's hand slipped out of his. With a start Boris looked at her. What was the matter? Nadia was staggering as if she had lost her balance. She tottered for a few steps, then she collapsed in the snow.

In a flash Boris was on his knees beside her.

'Nadia! Nadia!' He shouted her name and shook her, but she didn't respond. Her eyes were half-closed.

'Nadia! Nadia, do you hear me?' She couldn't just lie there. This couldn't be real. It mustn't be real.

The wind whirled over the ground and blew snow into her hair. Boris tried to make her sit up. He began to be afraid. Nadia surely wasn't going to die, like that old man who had just sunk down among the ruins? That couldn't happen. That musn't happen. 'Nadia. Nadia.' He said her name softly, pleading her to answer. Nadia, who was so brave and who knew where the potatoes were, Nadia couldn't die. Not now . . .

To his relief, he saw her lips move a little. She mumbled something, but Boris couldn't make out the words . . .

The horizon with the row of trees disappeared, as if a page of the white world had been turned over.

Far, far away, she heard Boris's voice. In a little while she'd speak to him, but now she just wanted to go to sleep. She couldn't do any more . . .

She felt Boris putting his arms round her. But she couldn't thank him. The whole world seemed to be growing tiny; black specks danced before her eyes . . .

There was Mother, standing at the stove making pancakes; the creamy batter sizzled in the iron pan.

There was Father, his brown eyes twinkling . . .
They were walking along the banks of the River Neva
and Serjozja had given her a balloon . . . There was
the Stipolevs' big dog, the one that had stolen her
doll and chewed it up . . .

Farther and farther she wandered into the little
world of her own memories. She was no longer aware
of Boris and their quest for potatoes; of starving
Leningrad, of beetroot soup that trickled away in the
snow . . .

The black spots dancing through her mind grew
bigger and bigger . . .

'Nadia!' Boris had unbuttoned his coat and pulled out
the old sack. He tried to push it under Nadia, but he
couldn't move her. What should he do? Despairingly he
looked around him. He couldn't leave her lying here in
the snow. He managed to get her partly on to the sack,
and fastened up her coat, which the wind had blown open.
What else could he do?

Boris pondered. Nadia's life depended on him, he knew
that. Could he drag her back to the city? Had he the
strength for that?

'Nadia, oh please, Nadia!' If only he could ask her
what he should do. But Nadia lay motionless. Perhaps
it would be best to try and find help. He could cover
Nadia with his coat. Boris started to get up, then stopped,
half-crouched, half-standing. His heart stood still. For
a moment he couldn't believe his eyes. He blinked. It
was still there – a boot, right next to him in the snow. And
above the boot, the rough green of a soldier's uniform.
And above that, the edge of a white cape. His heart
thumping, Boris let his gaze travel slowly upwards. There

was no doubt about it. Over an arm lay a rifle with a hand
on the trigger. And above . . .

Numb with fear, Boris stared into the face of a German
soldier . . .

His whole body trembled; for a moment he was too
shocked to think clearly. He just looked dazedly at the
German. What could he do to save Nadia and himself?
He could throw himself at the enemy's throat, and rid
himself of all his terror and grief and hate by strangling

50

this tall stranger. But he knew he wouldn't have a chance.

The soldier lowered his rifle. Boris crouched closer to the ground. Was he going to be beaten up? Would Nadia and he be flung into a concentration camp? What would happen to his mother? Tears of helpless rage sprang into his eyes. But his father had said he mustn't cry. And a German must never think that a young Russian was afraid. With a shaking hand he drew out the revolver in his pocket and pointed it at the soldier. Then he looked timidly up to see if the German was frightened by it. But the soldier showed no fear. He shook his head slowly from side to side; not angrily, not frowning, as you would have expected, but only slightly surprised, as if he knew quite well that the gun wasn't loaded. Disappointed, but also relieved, Boris let his hand drop.

'Du kleiner, was machst du hier?'

These were foreign words that Boris didn't understand, but they sounded friendly, almost gentle. Did the soldier want to know what they were doing there?

'We wanted to get potatoes,' said Boris and, because the German probably didn't understand Russian, he pointed to the row of trees in the distance and then to his mouth. The soldier would understand then that they hadn't come to fight them, but only to get food.

'Gott im Himmel!' muttered the soldier. He threw down his rifle, laid his hand on Boris's head, and knelt down by Nadia. Still confused, Boris looked at the rifle lying so close to his hands. Should he pick it up? If he was quick enough, he could shoot the soldier. That was what he had always wanted to do – to kill Germans. Weren't Germans everyone's hated enemies?

But from the way that the soldier was looking at Nadia,

from the way he put his arm round her and tried to make her sit up, Boris realized that he, at least, was no enemy. It was very bewildering.

'Ulli, Karl, Heinz, komm mal her!' called the soldier over his shoulder. With a start Boris looked round. Only then did he notice more Germans; their heads were sticking out from a ditch. They had pulled their white capes over themselves, so as not to be seen against the snowy background. Were they a small patrol, out reconnoitring? Or were there thousands of white-caped soldiers in the snow, preparing to launch a huge attack on Leningrad?

The three soldiers crawled out of the ditch and came up. They were carrying rifles and machine-guns.

Nadia stirred. Then her eyes opened. She had no idea where she was. Her great brown eyes were dazed. Slowly she turned her head and looked at the Germans. Boris saw her shrink back, and her eyes grew even bigger with fear.

'Boris!' Nadia tried to get up, but she was too weak.

'They're German soldiers,' Boris whispered helplessly.

'Hab keine Angst!' said the kneeling man, softly.

'Oh, Boris,' said Nadia. She shut her eyes and would have fallen back on the ground if the soldier had not held her tightly.

One of the other men took off his cape and pulled the haversack from his back. When he opened it Boris saw that it held a piece of sausage, and bread, and chocolate. His mouth watered. He watched the soldier break off a piece of chocolate and put it in Nadia's mouth.

Nadia gave a glimmer of a smile. The soldier nodded encouragingly at her. He gave her another piece and then another.

'Hier!' Another of the Germans was holding a piece of sausage right in front of Boris's nose. He looked at it longingly and then indecisively at the soldier. Could you accept anything from people who were enemies? How many tales of heroism had he heard about Russians who had refused to accept any such German bribes? He felt his hunger gnaw.

'Ist gut!' said the German.

Sorrowfully, Boris shook his head in refusal. He gulped. He realized just how tired he really was. The soldier seemed to sway before his eyes. Black spots danced among the snow.

'I must put my head down,' thought Boris, and he slid slowly on to the snow-covered ground.

7

Boris sat in the snow. He thought about his mother. What would she think if he never came home again? She would never know that he and Nadia had gone to No-man's-land to look for potatoes. No-man's-land — it was a foolish name, land of no man. And yet the Germans had come. He could hear their voices. The words that they spoke sounded hard and sharp. When he really began to listen to them, he could make out that there was some disagreement. He looked up in surprise. Yes, they were quarrelling, just like the children in Leningrad when they were playing at being at war, except that, he supposed, none of the Germans had wanted to play in the first place. Boris could not guess what this quarrel was about, but he could understand a few words: 'die Kinder . . .' and 'sterben . . .'

Nadia tried to sit up. With great frightened eyes she looked towards the Germans, who were still arguing fiercely among themselves.

'What are they saying, Nadia?' whispered Boris.

'They're talking about us,' answered Nadia.

Anxiously, Boris looked from one soldier to another. They were beginning to lose their tempers and their voices were getting louder and angrier. It seemed to be three against one.

'Es ist Wahnsinn! Ich geh nicht!' A soldier with a fair beard stamped his foot and walked moodily away in the direction of the row of trees. Boris stared after him tensely. What was going to happen? Dear God, the soldier who had wanted to give him the sausage had pulled his bayonet out. He fixed it into his rifle. Were they going to be tortured? Or were the Germans going to shoot them? Boris held his breath. A shiver of fear ran through his whole body.

But the soldier didn't stab them. He pulled a white handerkchief out of his pocket and tied it to the bayonet.

Then the miracle happened. The officer in charge came over to Nadia and picked her up in his arms. He pulled his cape round her. Next, Boris felt himself lifted up.

'Hab keine Angst!' said the soldier again. His voice sounded gentle and friendly. His kind blue eyes, which looked as if they were used to laughter, were sad now. They began to walk. The man with the handkerchief on the bayonet went ahead. He held his rifle in the air, so that the handkerchief fluttered in the wind.

'Boris . . . Boris . . .' called Nadia. It was a shout of joy. 'Boris, they're going to take us back to Leningrad!'

It was almost unbelievable, but they were going in the direction of the city. Again Boris looked at the face of the man who was carrying him. How was it possible that an enemy could have such a kind, friendly face?

'Ja, wir bringen euch nach Leningrad.' The

soldier smiled and nodded at Boris, as if to assure him that everything was going to be all right.

Now Boris could smile too. It was quite clear to him that these three Germans were friends, not enemies. He felt even more sorry now that he had refused that lovely piece of sausage. The boots crunched through the snow. Each stride brought them nearer to Leningrad. It was a comforting thought. Within a few hours he would be safe at home, if safe was a word that could still be used to describe any part of the besieged city . . .

After a good hour's marching, they came to a halt at the top of a long slope. Boris and Nadia were put down in the snow. Did the men want to have a rest? Their chests were heaving, and they stood to get their breath back, snorting like horses. They began to talk excitedly again, waving their hands in the air and pointing into the distance, where the black silhouette of Leningrad stood out clearly against the grey sky.

'What are they saying now?' whispered Boris.

'I think that they don't dare go any farther,' replied Nadia.

'Why not?'

'If our soldiers see that they're German, they'll shoot at once.'

Boris shuddered. Not for a moment had that thought occurred to him. He understood now why the soldier with the beard had stayed behind. It was not surprising that he feared the Russians.

'Do you think you could manage the last bit by yourself?' Boris asked anxiously. The Germans couldn't be expected to go any farther and there was still quite a way to go.

Nadia shrugged her shoulders. 'I don't know,' she murmured.

Alarm and uncertainty came flooding back with a great rush. His eyes wide with fear, Boris stared at the German soldiers. What would they decide? One of them was shaking his head — that was a bad sign.

'Hör mal zu!' ordered the officer. His face was grave but his voice was not angry. The others listened respectfully to those phrases so strange to the children's ears.

'Die Kinder . . . gefährlich . . . Leningrad . . . die Russen . . . schiessen . . . !'

Again Boris had the strongest feeling that these Germans were friends. In Leningrad everyone was convinced that all Germans were unfeeling murderers, that they killed helpless women and children without mercy, that they burned whole villages to the ground. Boris could not believe these three Germans capable of such horrors.

Once again the officer came over to them. Again a sad kind of smile appeared on his stern face. He slipped a piece of chocolate in each of their mouths.

How good it tasted! Boris shut his eyes tight so as not to lose a trace of the delightful creamy sweetness in his mouth.

'Thank you,' said Nadia politely, after a moment.

'Oh yes, thank you very much,' mumbled Boris. It was all right to accept presents from friends, he thought. It was just a pity that he couldn't take home a little bit of chocolate for his mother — especially as he'd be going back without any potatoes.

The Germans took off their white capes. They rolled them up neatly and pushed them between the straps of their haversacks. Boris couldn't think why they did that. They stood now in their green-grey uniforms, which looked all the darker and more noticeable against the snowy white background.

'Why did they do that?' Boris asked in a whisper.

Nadia shrugged her shoulders.

'Are they going to fight?' Perhaps it would be easier to fight without the long white capes.

'No,' said Nadia. 'The handkerchief on the rifle means that they don't intend to fight.'

'Are they going to take us any farther?'

'I think so,' said Nadia.

She was right. The officer came over to Boris and picked him up. He nodded to the children; for the first time his sad eyes looked slightly happy. One of the soldiers lifted Nadia in his arms.

'Jetzt gehen wir los!'

'Gott im Himmel,' muttered the soldier who was carrying the rifle with the handkerchief on it. He bit his lip, reluctant to go one step farther.

Once again the heavy boots crunched through the snow. They were walking now straight towards the Russian lines. That must take a lot of courage. Did these three German soldiers really know that so many people in Leningrad were dying of hunger? Did they realize how many men had drowned in Lake Ladoga? Did they know how many gunners dropped dead from sheer exhaustion behind their very guns? Bitter hate and a burning desire for revenge would greet them.

58

Boris peered anxiously into the distance. Would his fellow countrymen shoot as soon as they saw the three green German uniforms approaching over the snow? He was almost certain they would. In a fight for life or death there was no mercy. Could he warn his new friends about the danger? Or would that be treason against his own country? Boris tugged the officer's arm and pointed towards the Russian lines. 'Bang, bang!' he said, hoping the man would know what he meant.

'Danke! Ich weiss!' The officer nodded that he understood and once more smiled ruefully at Boris. He walked steadily on, like the brave soldier he was . . .

One shot rang out and then another. The German soldiers came to an abrupt halt. Tensely they stared into the distance. Boris held his breath. Was he going to see some action?

'Sie kommen!' grunted the officer in charge. He set Boris on the ground and gestured towards a forward post in the front line. At least fifteen Russian soldiers were to be seen approaching. They moved in close formation over the white ground, rifles at the ready.

'They've come to fetch us,' cried Nadia joyfully. Her brown eyes shone.

'Why did they shoot?' asked Boris. He was a bit uneasy.

'They were warning shots,' said Nadia. 'They didn't want the Germans to come too close to their lines.' She grasped Boris's hand and smiled at him. 'You needn't be afraid any longer.'

But Boris was afraid. The German soldier next to him, the one with the waving handkerchief tied to his rifle, raised the weapon higher in the air. He bit his lips nervously and the officer fingered his belt uncertainly. Were the Russians and the Germans going to fight? Fifteen against three isn't fair, thought Boris. Even the children in Leningrad had made each side equal in their war-games. But this was no game. Perhaps there was going to be fighting in real earnest.

With thumping heart Boris looked at the Russian

soldiers as they marched over the snow towards them. He was very happy to see them. But why did they look so stern and forbidding. Why did their grey-coated figures and their rifles look so menacing against the white background? It was impossible to read their thoughts or guess what their next actions would be.

A lieutenant walked on ahead. He was carrying a machine-gun, his right hand on the trigger. The earpieces of his fur cap flapped in the wind.

When they came to within about thirty yards, the Russian platoon spread out and formed a half-circle. And in this way they came up on three sides, with slow and threatening steps.

Boris swallowed. He gripped Nadia's hand, for they would soon know what was going to happen. For a moment he thought that Nadia was going to run to meet them, she looked so excited and happy. Didn't their stern, frowning faces discourage her at all? Why did none of the Russians seem pleased that they had got back safely?

When they had got right up to the Germans, the lieutenant held up his hand. The half-circle of his men stood motionless. There was absolute silence.

The officer in charge of the German patrol saluted and nodded a greeting to the Russians. But not one Russian returned his salute. Unmoving, they stared at their enemy. They would sooner kill them than smile at them, thought Boris.

A hopeless feeling of sorrow overwhelmed him. Why did everything have to be so complicated . . . ?

'Interpreter!' called the lieutenant.

An older man with glasses stepped forward.

'Ask them what they've come for.' His voice sounded

grim. The interpreter took another step forward and began to speak. He had some trouble with the harsh German words.

Boris peeped from under his cap at the Russians who stood around him. He saw distrust, hate, bitterness. Could no one begin to understand that these three Germans had shown themselves to be friends? The officer in charge gave his answer to the interpreter's question. Would he deign to tell them how kindly he had treated Nadia?

'They were on patrol in the forward lines,' said the interpreter to the Russian lieutenant, 'when they came across the children. The little girl had collapsed.'

The lieutenant looked sharply at Boris and Nadia. His eyes were hard and his voice abrupt.

'What's your name?'

'I'm Nadia Morozova,' Nadia murmured. She looked down at the ground. Everything seemed to be going so differently from what she had expected.

'And you?'

'My name's Boris . . . Boris Makarenko,' stammered Boris.

Why did the lieutenant look so stern? Was he angry because they had sneaked into No-man's-land? Or did he regard them as traitors – Russian children carried back in German arms? Boris hoped that Nadia would explain everything: about the air-raid, the rations, about his mother, about Serjozja who had died in the night. Surely the lieutenant would listen and understand.

'What were you doing so far outside the city?' The lieutenant looked sternly at Nadia again.

'We were looking for food,' Nadia said softly.

'Come here!' The lieutenant beckoned.

Nadia and Boris went over to him. They stood beside the Russians, facing the Germans. Two sides, one against the other. Between them lay six feet of No-man's-land, where no one had any identity. Boris couldn't bring himself to look at the German officer, he felt so ashamed of the Russian soldiers' determination to hide any human feelings.

'Ask him why they've brought back the children,' said the lieutenant to the interpreter.

Boris scraped the snow with his foot until the ground began to show. A few withered blades of grass still lingered in the frozen soil. Over his head the interpreter and the German officer exchanged question and answer.

'He says that the children had collapsed in the snow and were completely exhausted,' the interpreter translated into Russian. 'He says that even in an inhumane war people can show human feelings. Children have no part in the war. He couldn't find it in his heart to leave them lying in the snow. It was impossible to take them to the German lines. So he brought them here.'

Boris held his breath and looked anxiously at the lieutenant. Would he understand now that these were good Germans?

Suddenly the sergeant stepped forward. His voice was as cold as steel.

'Lieutenant,' he said, 'let's take away their guns. Maybe they have done a good deed; but maybe they're spies. Let's take them back and see if we can get any information out of them. After all that's happened, I've lost my faith in good Germans.'

Boris was filled with horror. He saw that the lieutenant was hesitating. Nadia pulled at his arm and looked fearfully at the sergeant.

'No, no, you can't do that,' she whispered. But no man standing in No-man's-land heard her speak.

'Don't believe a word they say,' put in another soldier from behind Nadia. His eyes gleamed with hatred. How much bitterness was bursting out of his heart?

'Shoot them right away, lieutenant. Shoot them right away.' Even as he spoke the man took a step forward and pointed his rifle at the German officer. Mad with hate, he meant to shoot . . .

Boris sprang forward. He ran to the German and stood

with his arms outstretched as if he could thus protect him.

'Don't shoot,' he yelled, his voice breaking. 'Don't shoot. They saved our lives.'

It was deathly silent. No one said a word. No one moved.

'Come here,' commanded the lieutenant. But Boris didn't come. He stood firmly in front of the German. A desperate, helpless wave of passion swept over him; tears of rage against the hatred, terror and madness of war filled his eyes.

'Nadia was lying in the snow.' Boris screamed the words at the Russian. 'She couldn't even speak to me. I couldn't carry her. I tried to, but I couldn't.' He jerked his head at the German behind him. 'He carried her. He's my friend.' Frantically Boris tried to make them understand. 'My friend, do you hear – my friend!' He was crying with rage.

Nadia came over to him.

'Boris, Boris dear,' she said gently, but Boris shook with sobs.

Then Boris felt a firm hand on his shoulder, a friendly hand. He looked up into the German's face. Through his tears he saw the officer smiling at him. At once the terror began to fade from his tearful eyes.

Then Boris looked at the lieutenant. The harshness on his face had given way to astonishment. The soldier who had wanted to shoot had lowered his rifle and was scraping it idly in the snow; some of the other soldiers were gazing into the distance. The sergeant stared at Nadia. Again no one said a word . . .

Then the lieutenant turned to the interpreter. 'Tell them they are free to go back, Ivan Petrovitch.' He hesitated, as if searching for words. 'Say to them that we are grateful; it would be shameful if we, in the brutality of war, should forget all humanity.'

The interpreter translated his words.

The German soldiers made to turn on their heels, but the officer remained as he was.

'Ein Augenblick, bitte!' He pulled his haversack from his shoulder and stopped to open it.

'Hier,' he said to Boris and Nadia, and handed them each a piece of bread and sausage, and a tin with foreign words on the label.

66

Once again Boris felt that trustworthy hand on his shoulder. Then the officer stood up straight. Slowly he looked round the watching circle, with that same sad smile that Boris had already seen on his face, clapped his heels together and saluted. He stood as stiff and straight as a candle, the typical German soldier.

The young lieutenant of the Red Army stood smartly to attention. 'Platoon,' he ordered, 'attention!' All the Russians sprang to attention. Slowly the lieutenant brought his hand up to his cap. It was as if he were saluting the Germans for their courage, their help, their humanity.

Boris looked at the officer. He would have liked to thank him again, but the German had turned on his heel. With firm steps he and the others walked away down the slope into the distance: men in No-man's-land.

Nadia waved hesitantly, but the Germans did not look back.

The snow-covered land no longer lay like an unwritten page under the grey sky. The prints of German boots had written a message on it for all to read . . .

In the advance post, Nadia and Boris were each given a mug of scalding tea and half a corned-beef sandwich. They felt very lucky to get the food and drink, because the soldiers' rations did not amount to very much, though they were allowed more than civilians. If the troops weren't fed, there wouldn't be a hope of maintaining the fight.

A kettle hung on a hook in a fire-place made of sandbags. The place was just like a witch's cave. In a few minutes Boris felt his cheeks begin to glow. The lieutenant tramped up and down restlessly. From his drawn brows it was clear that something was troubling him. Every so often he looked as if he were about to speak, but then his glance would fall on Nadia, and he would change his mind. Was he waiting until they had finished their tea and bread? Boris began to eat more quickly. He nudged Nadia to make her do the same, for she seemed to be just playing with her sandwich, nibbling tiny little bits of it, as if she could only swallow a crumb at a time.

'Eat up,' whispered Boris. Didn't she know that a lieutenant of the Red Army couldn't be kept waiting for long? The two of them were certainly in for a scolding, if not a severe punishment. All the same, Boris was not in the least sorry that he had gone with Nadia. Under his jacket sat the bread and the sausage that the German officer had given him. Mother would have a fine supper that evening, unless . . . In sudden panic Boris glanced at the lieutenant. But he was now leaning thoughtfully against a pile of empty crates, and stared only at the ground. Surely he would not take away the food as a punishment? The lieutenant looked up and Boris guiltily dropped his eyes. Almost against his will he pressed his arm against his jacket, as if to shield the bread and sausage.

The lieutenant came over and stood in front of him. 'How did you get to the forward lines?' he asked.

Because Nadia had at that moment put the piece of bread into her mouth and was dreamily staring into space, not even seeing or hearing the lieutenant, Boris was forced to answer.

'We went under the bridge. Then we went farther along the river-bank. There was a hole in the barbed-wire netting . . .'

The lieutenant looked at Nadia. 'Did your mother and father know where you were going?'

Nadia still didn't say a word. Boris thought he knew why she was silent.

'She hasn't got a father any longer,' he said quietly. The lieutenant shook his head. Now Boris could see that he wasn't angry – he just looked very grave.

'How did you know the way?'

'Serjozja, her big brother, told Nadia,' said Boris, hesitating slightly.

'And why didn't her big brother go for himself?'

Boris didn't dare look at Nadia. 'Serjozja died the night before,' whispered Boris, hoping that Nadia still wasn't listening.

Silence fell in the cramped room. The lieutenant had turned his back to them. Boris peeped sideways at Nadia; at once he saw that she was looking a bit queer. She was leaning to the side against a sand-bag, and her eyes were staring wildly again.

'Nadia,' called Boris, frightened, but not so frightened as he had been the first time she had collapsed. The lieutenant acted quickly. He snapped an order at the soldier who was standing guard outside the door, and bent over Nadia. He unbuttoned her coat and laid his ear on her chest.

'That's how she lay in the snow,' said Boris.

An engine started up outside. A soldier came to report that there was a van standing ready. The lieutenant wrapped Nadia in a blanket and picked her up as if she were a doll. She couldn't be much heavier, thought Boris, she was so thin.

'Go like lightning to Dr. Ilya Ivanov,' said the lieutenant. Of course, he himself had to stay on duty, in case the Germans attacked.

As he walked along the narrow track to the waiting van, Boris realized just how tired he was. He felt like lying down where he was and going to sleep. But he couldn't; he had to go with Nadia. When he felt himself lifted into the truck he remembered with satisfaction that the lieutenant hadn't punished them, and that the bread and sausage had passed unnoticed . . .

They were driven through the fighting lines: long rows of barbed wire, tanks, look-out posts. Even though he was dead tired Boris was still intrigued by the machine-gun posts, the huge gun turrets, the trenches . . .

'One day I'll be marching up and down here,' he thought. But it didn't seem so marvellous now. He thought about the three Germans who had brought

Nadia and him to the Russian lines. If you were a soldier you had to kill good Germans along with bad. You certainly couldn't know which kind you were aiming at. What if one day he were to kill the commander of the patrol who had saved them? The thought troubled Boris. He didn't think he wanted to be a soldier after all.

The van stopped in front of a small wooden building. The soldier had brought Nadia to Dr. Ilya Ivanov, a short man with glasses, who swore under his breath when he saw Nadia. Since no one forbade it, Boris went in with her. In a tiny waiting-room he sat down on a bench, next to a soldier with a hand wrapped in a blood-stained bandage. The place smelled of disinfectant, like a hospital. Boris didn't like to look too closely at that bandage. It looked as if the hand was very badly damaged. But he had to look in its direction because the soldier began to talk to him.

'How do you come to be here, young fellow?'

Boris told him what had happened.

'You mean to tell me those pigs brought you back to our lines?' The soldier almost forgot his wounds in astonishment.

'They were good Germans,' declared Boris.

'The only good Germans are dead Germans,' retorted the soldier. He gingerly supported his wounded hand with his sound one. Boris would have loved to tell him how the officer had knelt by Nadia in the snow — he wanted to make him understand that he had been a good German. But it looked as if this was not the moment to argue.

'Is it very painful?'

The soldier shrugged his shoulders.

'Did the . . .' Boris hesitated . . . 'Did the Germans do that?'

The soldier nodded. The pain in his eyes turned to hatred. 'We were on patrol. The rotters were lying in a ditch with their white capes covering them. We didn't see them until it was too late.' He stared at the bloodstained bandage. 'I didn't have any luck,' he muttered, half to himself. He stared through the tiny window into the distance.

Boris shivered. A horrid feeling crept over him. Could it have been his good German who had shot at the soldier?

'How many were there?' he whispered.

'Four,' answered the soldier. 'And we didn't get one of them.'

Sad and ashamed, Boris looked at the floor. What on earth would the soldier think of him? Could an enemy ever be a friend? And yet they were good Germans. But how could you explain that to a soldier whose hand had been half-shot away?

Boris just didn't know what he could say to him. Fortunately the door to the surgery opened. Dr. Ilya Ivanov let out the van-driver who still carried Nadia in his arms. Thank God! Her eyes were open and she looked more like herself.

'Now, remember, do exactly as I've told you,' said the doctor, pinching her cheek. Then he nodded to the wounded soldier to come inside.

'Are you feeling better again?' said Boris.

'Yes,' said Nadia. 'I had an injection.'

'Did it hurt?'

'Only a little bit.' She didn't add that the doctor had

had to prick her arm several times before he had found the right place. He had said that it was because her arms were so scraggy.

Once again they were lifted into the truck and the soldier started the engine. Boris sat close up to Nadia. Everything was all right now. He could look forward to getting home with his bread and sausage and his tin.

The drive through the streets seemed to go on for ever. They had often to go back the way they had come because the road was blocked. That morning's air-raid had hit the city hard, and here and there small flames still danced among the smouldering, smoking ruins . . .

Dusk began to fall, but everywhere men, women and children were still hard at work. At the corner of one burning street was heaped a pile of furniture. A woman sat bewildered among her belongings. Two men carried a stretcher to an ambulance. Boris thought of his mother. Would she be very worried because he was so late getting home? Terrible things were happening — but that their own house should be struck was simply unthinkable. That was something he wouldn't and couldn't consider.

They had to go all the way past the Winter Palace and along the windy bank of the River Neva before they could turn down towards where they lived. At last they came to their own street. The soldier slowed down. They drove past Victor Zorov's house and the place where Stipolev used to live.

'This is where Boris lives,' said Nadia. The van stopped. The soldier opened the door and Boris clambered on to the running-board.

'Good-bye, and thanks for bringing me home,' he

said. He looked at Nadia. Perhaps he ought to go with her, or would the soldier take good care of her? Nadia smiled at him, a special secret smile. Boris smiled back. He was quite sure that he would ask Nadia to marry him when he grew up.

'Good-night, Boris,' said Nadia.

'Good-night, Nadia,' answered Boris. He jumped down. The soldier slammed the door and the van drove off.

Slowly Boris went indoors. Afterwards, a long time afterwards, he was to be sorry that he hadn't said more, much more, than just good-night . . .

10

Uncle Vanya was there. Boris saw him as soon as he went into the room. Solid as a boulder, he sat on the chair beside his mother's bed. He got up when he saw Boris.

'Confound it, boy,' he roared. Uncle Vanya always roared – that was his way of being friendly. 'Where have you been? Did you get lost?'

Mother raised herself up on her pillows. She had been crying, and this time she didn't bother to pretend she hadn't been.

'Boris, oh Boris,' she murmured. She held out her arms and smiled joyfully through her tears.

'Young rascal,' growled Uncle Vanya. He pushed Boris over to the bed so that his mother could give him a hug. She held him so tightly that Boris was bewildered – and worried, in case she felt the bread and sausage and the tin.

'The raid was over a long time ago, but you didn't come,' said his mother softly.

'She thought you'd been killed and were lying under a heap of rubble!' Uncle Vanya, half-vexed, half-relieved, put his arm around Boris's shoulder.

'But I'd told you that I was going with Nadia,' Boris said.

'But you didn't say where you and Nadia were going to,' boomed Uncle Vanya. 'You might have been in Linow Street.'

'What's going on there?' asked Boris.

Uncle Vanya looked at him with his kindly eyes and shook his head.

'There isn't a Linow Street any longer. It got a direct hit. If you'd been there . . .'

Boris nodded. He realized now why his mother had been so worried. Slightly ashamed, he gazed at Uncle Vanya's moustache, which seemed to be drooping even more mournfully than usual. And his face had become much more wrinkled recently. He must have come to discuss the evacuation question. Had he promised to put Boris's name on the list? Would he be forced to ride in that terrible convoy over Lake Ladoga?'

'I came across some food when I was with Nadia,' said Boris quickly. He had to let them see, as quickly as possible, that he was no longer a child. With shaking fingers he undid his coat. Without a word, he placed the bread, the sausage and the tin on the table next to the bed. There, that gave them a surprise, no doubt about it.

'Good Lord!' exclaimed Uncle Vanya. 'Where on earth did you get that?' He picked up the sausage in his huge hand and gazed at it in astonishment. 'You can't find a piece of this in the whole of Leningrad.'

'I got it from a German,' said Boris.

They stared at him in astonishment. Then he told them how he and Nadia had gone into No-man's-land, what a long and icy way they had had to walk, how Nadia had at last collapsed in the snow, and how he had seen that big German boot right next to him as he lay exhausted beside her.

'Crazy child, crazy!' muttered Uncle Vanya.

Boris went on with his story. He saw that his words were having effect, for Uncle Vanya and his mother kept glancing at each other significantly. Did they understand now that he was much too big and brave to be sent away? But when he had told the whole story, the words of admiration he expected to hear failed to come out.

'Boris,' said his mother softly. Tears were in her eyes again and her fingers plucked nervously at the blanket. Boris didn't know why. Surely there was no need to cry now? His mother made as if to pull him towards her, but Uncle Vanya laid his hand on Boris's shoulder.

'Now, you'd better listen to me, my lad,' he said sternly. 'Your mother and I have been talking about you for a long time today. We've decided to send you to stay with a cousin of ours – Olga Petrovna, who lives in Sverdlovsk.'

Boris didn't believe it. Sverdlovsk was miles and miles away from Leningrad. Hundreds of miles. The thought of going there gave him such a shock that he simply couldn't say a word; a lump came into his throat. He fixed his eyes on the bread and sausage. Wasn't the food evidence that he wasn't a child any longer?

It was as if time had stopped in the room. Would neither of them say that it wasn't true? At last –

'It really is better this way, darling,' said his mother. She held out her hand. 'Olga Petrovna is very kind. You'll have a good time at her home.'

'But . . . what about you?' Boris swallowed hard.

'I'm going to go and stay with Uncle Vanya.'

'And this house?'

'When the war is over, we'll come back here again,' said his mother, with that glimpse of a smile that Boris knew so well. It always appeared when there was no reason in the world to look happy.

'I'll take care of all the details about your journey,' said Uncle Vanya.

'I'm not going,' said Boris firmly. 'I won't go.'

'No one says "won't" in a war, my lad.' Uncle Vanya's voice sounded more gentle than Boris had ever heard it. 'Any will of our own has been shot dead by the German guns.'

'I don't care. I won't go.' Boris looked obstinate.

'No one wants things like this to happen, but still they happen.' Uncle Vanya pulled Boris against him. 'No woman wants the man she married to go to the front line. But he goes. No man wants his wife to die of hunger. But it happens. Every Russian must do things that he hates doing because it is necessary.' Uncle Vanya looked into Boris's eyes. 'And now it's necessary for you to go to Sverdlovsk.'

'Let the other children go first.'

'We haven't any choice, Boris. No one has any choice.'

Boris looked at his mother, hoping for some support from her. But when he saw her face, he realized that there was nothing more to say – he would have to go. She looked so white and fragile. He couldn't refuse the appeal in her eyes.

'Olga Petrovna is so kind,' said his mother, but she couldn't stop her hands from trembling. She was more upset than Boris, and he would only make it harder for her if he kept on arguing. If he kept on saying that he would never go, then his mother would have to cope with yet another burden. His grief was her grief, his pain was her pain.

'I must be brave,' thought Boris. 'I must spare her some pain, just as she's trying to do for me.'

Uncle Vanya stood up. 'I must go now,' he said. He gave Mother a kiss and once more clapped Boris's shoulder.

'I'll see that everything is in order.' Boris nodded. He did his best to smile, but it was very difficult.

78

Boris had fallen asleep in his chair. While they had eaten the German's bread and sausage, his mother had told him about long ago, when she and Olga Petrovna had played together as children. Boris had been so tired that he couldn't keep his eyes open. He didn't know that his mother had got out of her bed and helped him into his. He hadn't felt her light touch on his forehead as she kissed him good-night.

11

Next morning it was freezing hard. Boris felt the cold hit him in the face when he went with his pan to get the rations at the canteen. His nose and throat tingled, and it was painful to breathe.

The minute he had wakened, Boris had remembered about being sent away. With this bitter cold, Lake Ladoga would soon be completely frozen. Before Christmas the lorries would be on their way again; and then he would have to leave Leningrad with the children. Angrily Boris kicked a piece of ice out of the way. He must think of some way of avoiding evacuation. Perhaps Nadia would have a plan. He stood and waited for a while in front of her house. He would tell her everything on the way to the canteen. He couldn't discuss it with his mother; it was a hard enough thought for her to bear already, as Boris knew very well. Uncle Vanya: he was all right as an uncle – good fun and generous, even if his moustache did droop . . . but . . .

'I'm not going,' Boris muttered to himself. 'Whatever happens, I'm not going.' He would rather starve to death than travel in one of those lorries across the lake.

Nadia would know a way out. But Nadia didn't appear. Boris looked idly along the street. Diagonally opposite was a gap where Ivan and Nina's house had been burned down. An incendiary bomb must have fallen just there. He thought sadly about the times when he had played with Ivan. How would he be getting on in the orphanage behind Nevskiy Prospekt?

Perhaps Nadia had already left. At any rate, it was too cold to hang about and Boris began to walk on slowly. He kept on looking over his shoulder in the hope that he would see Nadia coming after him. From far away he heard the sound of gunfire. Was the German officer trying to slip through No-man's-land to attack the Russians?

Boris came to the square with its statues entombed in sand-bags. Roadmen were busy filling up the crater that the previous day's bomb had left. Two heavily laden lorries were parked half-across the pavement. Lorries . . . !

'Whatever happens I will not go and stay with Olga Petrovna,' said Boris to himself again. Even if no one had any choice any longer, as Uncle Vanya had said, he was still sure he wouldn't go. It was a comforting feeling to know that for certain . . .

There was a long queue outside the canteen. For the most part it was women and children who stood waiting so patiently, but Nadia was not there. Boris took his place at the end of the queue. He listened to the remarks being made – that helped to pass the time.

'It's bitter cold.'

'You can say that again.'

'If the lake freezes, we'll have a chance of some extra rations.'

'Perhaps the soup will get thicker.'

'Thicker and richer.'

Boris hoped from the bottom of his heart that it would thaw, even if he was wishing away rich thick soup.

If only he didn't have to go to Sverdlovsk. Once more

he looked behind him to see if Nadia had arrived, but she wasn't there.

'They're holding out well in Stalingrad.'

'Just like us.'

'My husband says the offensive's bound to begin soon. Then they'll come and liberate us.'

'It won't last much longer – we can't go on like this indefinitely.'

These were words that Boris had heard a hundred times. It won't last much longer . . . But things that you longed for didn't always happen. Boris lost interest and scraped the snow idly with his foot. What a pity Nadia hadn't come!

Foot by foot the queue shuffled forward.

'Any news of your husband?'

'Not a word.'

'I've put the children's names on the list. What will become of them?'

'It can't last much longer.'

'We've been saying that for so long now.'

'But they're still holding out in Stalingrad.'

How easy it was to forget, thought Boris, that the war was going on outside Leningrad. Stalingrad . . . Moscow . . . Like a tidal wave war was sweeping through the land; like a forest fire it raged onwards.

Nadia still hadn't come. Slowly but steadily Boris was moving up to the counter where the soup was being served. Would it be beetroot soup yet again? Now it was the turn of the woman just in front of him. Boris craned forward to see what was in the ladle. It was beetroot, and it was less thick than the day before. The woman looked at it blankly. She shook her head, as if she didn't know why she had stood so long in the queue, for such thin watery soup. Then she laughed and looked up at the cook.

'Tomorrow it'll be melted snow you'll be giving us.' It was a poor joke.

The man laughed back. 'Snow-soup and maybe a lump of ice extra. What more could anyone want?'

The woman laughed again, but it wasn't a happy laugh.

'It's not very much, but it's the best I can do,' said the cook.

The woman picked up her pan with a sigh and went out.

Boris put his pan on the table and handed over his ration card. The cook had the same little rash round his lips as his mother. Even though you were a cook it seemed you still didn't get enough to eat . . .

It was starting to snow again as Boris set off for home. At every street corner he was met by a flurry of snowflakes blown in all directions by the wind. A white veil was being drawn over the city. The world grew stiller, smaller, more mysterious. Even the distant gunfire faded.

When he came to Nadia's house, Boris paused. In the end he thought he'd have a look through the windows on the ground floor. No one to be seen; nothing unusual. He had expected that Nadia would be at her window watching the snowflakes. She liked doing that. As she looked at the whirling flakes, she would imagine all sorts of things – the snowflakes were racing each other to see which reached the ground first. Why did the snow fall? Nadia would say that the stars were tired of looking at the ground and wanted to make it look prettier.

It was a pity he had missed Nadia, but he really couldn't wait any longer. The snow began to get thicker.

'If I stand here much longer I'll be a snowman,' decided Boris, and the only advantage of being a snowman was that he couldn't be sent to Olga Petrovna's house in Sverdlovsk.

Boris gave one last hopeful look at Nadia's window, then made for home . . .

With wood that Uncle Vanya had brought Boris made a fire and warmed up the soup. They were so hungry that it tasted wonderful. Afterwards they played three games of chess and each time he beat his mother.

'You've never played so badly before,' he accused her.

'Perhaps it is you who have never played so well.'

But Boris knew better than that. Her thoughts had been far away from chess.

Afterwards Boris made a start on his homework, which he'd brought back from school before the Christmas holidays. He hadn't done very much.

It was dark early that evening because the sky was still heavy with snow. They went to bed early. Boris thought that this was the best hour of the day – it was the only time he was really warm enough and then he and his mother would talk about everything and anything.

'Tell me again what it used to be like.' His mother smiled in the darkness. She knew just what it was that Boris wanted to hear. She began to describe the great estate where she and Uncle Vanya had been brought up. There were as many as thirty farms on the estate and they had all belonged to his grandfather.

As mother told the story he could see the big house coming to life in the early morning; hear the voices of the servants and the sharp French accent of the governess. He could smell the crisp fresh bread as it was taken piping hot out of the ovens; the tea in the samovar standing in the dining-room, where Grandfather sat at the head of the table, frowning when Uncle Vanya helped himself to too much jam.

'Just as we were finishing breakfast, we would hear bells tinkling as Casimir brought the *droschka* round. Then it was time to go to school.' Casimir was the coachman, with a sheepskin coat reaching to his feet. In front of the sledge stood Poesjka and Flom, the two greys. Mother didn't need to go on – Boris knew it all. In his imagination he could see everything for himself: the huge hall, with deers' antlers and boars' tusks on the walls, trophies of Grandfather's hunting days. In the hall the governess waited to help them on with their coats. They always said, 'Merci, Mademoiselle!' because she came from France. Mother and Uncle Vanya kissed Grandfather good-bye and then they got into the sledge. They sat at the back, well covered up with thick rugs. And then Casimir would crack the whip . . .

Boris heaved a sigh. What a marvellous way to go to school!

That night his mother told him about the great day when his grandfather had summoned all his tenants and given them the freehold of their land. For his grandfather was one of the first Russians to believe that all men should be equal.

'The men cried for joy, Boris. Like all Russians, they weren't afraid to show their feelings. You should have seen how they each came up in turn to kiss Grandfather's hand.'

But soon the first world war broke out. War even then! Grandfather had marched to the front line to fight for Russia against the Germans. He had never come back . . .

A few years later the great Revolution had swept through the land. That was when Mother had seen Father for the first time.

'He marched through the streets of Leningrad in a parade of hundreds of men. Father led them, bearing the red flag. He looked marvellous – so gay, so full of hope
86

for the new world, where all men would live in peace and happiness.'

But other people had other ideas, and so civil war had broken out. Five million people died of hunger. Hunger even then! And now there was another war. How many men would fight, how many women would weep, how many children would be sent away from home before the guns would be silent for ever?

'Only the snowflakes know the answer.' That's what Nadia would have said. 'But they're so sad about it that they turn to tears before they reach the earth.'

Some day, someone would find the answer, but it seemed a long way away to Boris.

'Tell me about what you used to do at Easter,' he said quickly. And his mother described once again how they had gone to church, with bells ringing all along the way and the people waving and calling out good wishes.

But what these wishes were Boris did not hear. He had fallen asleep, to dream of his father marching with the red flag through the streets of Leningrad.

12

The following morning it was still snowing. There had been quite a thick fall during the night Boris noticed

when he went outside. Here and there warmly wrapped-up women were bent over their work of clearing the snow; a mantle of white covered their heads and shoulders. Men couldn't be spared now for this work. With brooms and wooden spades the women shovelled the snow from the pavement in front of the houses. Slowly a narrow path was being dug out along the pavement.

Again Boris stood waiting in vain for Nadia. Was she already on her way to the canteen? Boris began to run. He hoped he would catch up with her. He had to talk to her about Sverdlovsk. He decided that if he didn't see her before, he would go up to her house on the way home. He walked on feeling a bit happier. Leningrad looked less ugly under the snow. You couldn't see the devastation. The ruined houses and the statues, muffled in their sand-bags, were like snow castles.

Thank goodness it's snowing, thought Boris. Now at least they could be sure that there wouldn't be an air-raid . . .

Slowly Boris climbed up the stairs to the first floor. He left his pan of soup in the entrance downstairs where no one could see it. He didn't like the idea of ringing Nadia's doorbell. Should he say anything to her mother about her father and brother? Should he say how dreadful it must be for her?

Boris pulled the bell. He heard it ring, but no one came to open the door. He rang again, then looked at the stair-way. He thought about all the games he had played here with Nadia. Real Nadia-games. One of their favourites was 'Knock-knock'. You started at the top stair and for each good answer you jumped down a step. The one who reached the bottom step first was the winner.

'Knock, Knock!'
'Who's there?'
'Rose!'
'Rose what?'
'Rows of little houses.'

There were twenty-two steps. But you always had to ask about forty nonsense questions before you reached the bottom. They had always laughed so much – in fact, once, Nadia had nearly fallen all the way down.

Boris rang the bell a third time, but still no one answered.

Disappointed, Boris went slowly down the twenty-two steps to the ground floor. He picked up his pan and went outside. It was still snowing. If you looked long enough at the sky, the whirling snowflakes made you feel quite dizzy – the snowflakes that, according to Nadia, knew why there was a war . . .

When he got home, Uncle Vanya was sitting beside his mother's bed. He had brought official papers for her to sign. Four times she filled in her signature, in her still clear and flowing hand.

'So that's everything taken care of,' said Uncle Vanya. He stood up and put the papers back in the envelope.

'Aren't you staying?' asked Boris. But Uncle Vanya shook his head.

'I'm much too busy. There's such a lot to be done.'

A hasty kiss for Mother, a clap on the shoulder for Boris, and Uncle Vanya had gone.

'Is he busy seeing about the children who are to be evacuated?' asked Boris.

Mother nodded. 'If he could, Uncle Vanya would try to protect the whole world. But since he can't do that, he's doing his best to look after every single child in Leningrad.'

'I wonder if he ever thinks that the children might not like that,' muttered Boris, drawing his brows together.

'What did you say?' asked his mother.

'They might not want to be looked after by Uncle Vanya.'

Mother looked at him very seriously, so that Boris began to feel sorry for his last words.

'They might not know now that he was doing it for their own good,' she said quietly. 'But later, much later, when they're men and women, they'll realize how fortunate they were that Uncle Vanya was here to look after them.'

Boris nodded silently, but he still thought with loathing about the prospect of Sverdlovsk.

'Perhaps the children who are evacuated will one day be famous scientists or doctors, who will also save lives. Or perhaps they'll be writers whose books will give pleasure to thousands. One of them one day might be President.'

'And will he see that war never happens again?'

'Who knows?' said his mother, with a sad little smile.

Boris sat and thought for a long time about what she had said. But he himself didn't yet quite know what he wanted to be when he grew up, so it didn't seem necessary that Uncle Vanya should take so much trouble over protecting him. Whatever happened, he wanted to stay with his mother. Therefore it was absolutely necessary to talk to Nadia. She would certainly be able to think of some way of getting round this evacuation business, even though all the documents were signed.

It was late in the afternoon by the time Boris went back

to Nadia's house. Slowly the last of the snowflakes danced down on Leningrad. The sky began to grow lighter. It felt as if it was going to freeze really hard. Once again Boris went up the twenty-two steps. Once again he rang the bell. He rang once, twice, and then a third time, hard and long. Still the house was silent. An icy shiver ran through Boris – had something happened . . . ?

Farther along the landing a door opened. Irina Akimova, the old woman who lived next door, came shuffling along carrying a big water-jug.

'Are you looking for Nadia?' she inquired.

'Yes,' said Boris.

'Have you rung the bell?'

'Three times just now, and this morning too.'

Boris thought Irina Akimova was going to let the jug fall. She threw an alarmed glance at the closed door. Then she stared at Boris. She put down the jug and clutched at the door-frame for support.

'Yuri, Yuri,' she called, her voice rising with excitement. 'Yuri, quickly!'

'What's the matter?' Yuri appeared at the door. He looked at them sleepily. Irina Akimova pointed at the door. The terror on her face made words unnecessary.

Boris's heart began to beat faster. His breath caught in his throat. He didn't want to think about, didn't want to see, what lay behind that closed door. It was too terrible to imagine – but nothing was too terrible in this war.

'Nadia,' he whispered, without hearing his own voice. His eyes dropped to the treads of the stairs. Nadia, Nadia, Nadia. He could see her jumping up and down and hear her light, happy voice asking nonsense questions.

Behind him, Yuri Akimov broke open the door. Boris

saw Nadia's coat hanging in the narrow passage. Serjozja's shoes lay under a table.

Yuri Akimov looked at his wife. Boris understood clearly the message in their eyes. He could not bear to watch.

Irina pushed him aside and walked into the room.

'Dear God in Heaven!'

Yuri put his hand to his heart and then slowly made the sign of the cross.

Boris stood like stone in the passage. He knew he might as well go away again, for he didn't need to be told that there was nothing now that he could say to Nadia. But he couldn't believe it. Nadia! It couldn't be! It was impossible. Then suddenly there was no trace of doubt, only cold certainty.

Irina Akimova came slowly out of the room.

'Are they . . . ?' Yuri couldn't go on.

Irina nodded. In her hand she carried a thick blue notebook. She held it out.

'While she was writing this!'

She laid the notebook on the table, directly above Serjozja's shoes. It was Nadia's diary . . .

Boris never knew how long he stood on the stair landing. People walked backwards and forwards past him. Doors opened and shut. An old woman hobbled down the stairs. She was carrying an ikon with a picture of the Holy Trinity. She was clutching a stump of candle. Was she going to burn it for Nadia and her mother. Why all this fuss, thought Boris – if you were dead you weren't there any longer. He didn't dare go inside. Yet he couldn't bring himself to go home. It was as if the day had broken in pieces and he couldn't put the bits together again.

Softly he crept to the door where the women were going in and out. Then he saw Nadia's diary lying on the small table just inside. No one paid any attention to him. Sad, whispered voices and sobs came from the bedroom.

Boris gazed at Serjozja's big empty shoes and tears rolled down his cheeks. Through a mist he read the words on the cover of the blue notebook: Nadia Morozova's Diary.

No one saw him hastily pick up the notebook and stuff it under his jacket. Quickly he tiptoed out of the room and down the stairs. Each tread seemed to call out a question:

'Why Nadia?'

'Why Nadia and not Boris?'

'Why had Uncle Vanya not saved her in time?'

'Who would now tell him what to do about Sverdlovsk?'

'Why Nadia?' The question echoed and re-echoed.

With the diary tightly clutched under his coat, Boris walked along the narrow path between the banks of snow to his house. He kept on looking at the sky. It was certainly going to freeze hard. All the snow-clouds had vanished and the sky was clear and blue. Boris wondered if Nadia were somewhere watching him . . .

13

When Boris got back to his own house, he didn't say anything to his mother. He simply couldn't face it. Nadia was dead; that was a raw, still open wound that you mustn't touch, or else you would scream with pain. When he laid Nadia's diary on the table, his mother asked:

'What is that?'

'Oh, just a notebook.'

Boris tried hard not to think of Nadia, of her mother, of her diary. He wanted to forget how Nadia's coat and hood had been hanging on the hallstand, and how Serjozja's big, thick shoes had lain under the table. When he had been going about the house doing his various jobs it hadn't been so bad . . . But now he was lying in bed. Now his thoughts came crowding in on him: whether he wished it or not, he kept on thinking about Nadia, who had fallen asleep for ever while she was writing her diary . . . Boris felt the sobs inside him grow bigger until they almost choked him . . . He could almost see Nadia sitting writing, sometimes hesitating because she was too tired to think of the right word, then writing a few words more, at last letting the pencil fall . . .

All at once Boris began to cry. He bit his lips, hoping his mother wouldn't hear. A sob came, and then another . . .

'Boris?'

He couldn't answer. Silently he fought his tears.

'Boris!'

Boris gave in and wept openly. He heard rustling and soft footsteps, then he felt his mother's hand on his forehead.

'Boris, what's the matter?'

He shook his head. He didn't want to talk about it. Not yet. Mother bent over him and drew him towards her.

'Tell me about it,' she said gently. 'It will be much better if you tell me what's wrong.'

All his misery and pain burst out, and Boris sobbed in his mother's arms.

'Nadia is dead.'

For a moment all was still. Boris felt his mother's hand stiffen on his back.

'Oh, my dear, my dear!' Her voice was gentle and sad, yet comforting. 'Poor little Nadia.'

'Why did she have to die?' Mother's hand now lay calm and firm on his shoulder.

'When people we love die, Boris, we always want to know why. But we may not ask that question. We must go on living our own lives, and as we grow older we begin to find out the answer for ourselves.'

'But how?'

'By living to do the things that our hearts and our hands find to do. For each other, for Russia, for the whole world.'

Mother sighed and gave a shiver. It was cold in the room, because the stove was lit only during the day.

'You go back to bed,' said Boris. 'You'll catch cold.'

He felt his mother's hand stroke his hair. Then she stood up. But she didn't go towards the bed. In the dim light he saw her going over to the dresser. He heard her looking for something among the stuff that lay on it. The matches! He heard the box rattle. Then his mother went

96

to her bed. She put something on the small table and struck a match.

At last Boris saw what his mother was doing. On the table next to her bed stood a silver candlestick with their last candle in it which Mother had been saving for Christmas. Beside it lay the notebook.

Mother lit the candle and got into bed.

'What are you going to do?' asked Boris in surprise.

'Come in beside me,' said Mother. 'We'll read Nadia's diary together.'

Reluctantly Boris came over to the big bed. He didn't want his mother to read the diary. The wound was still too painful to be touched.

'We cannot hide our eyes when things like this happen,' said his mother after Boris lay beside her.

At that moment the sirens began to wail . . .

Months ago, Boris and his mother had made up their minds that when the sirens went during the night they would not go to the shelter.

'There's no point in it – what will be, will be,' his mother had said.

Since then they had just stayed in bed when the sirens sounded. The first time Boris had felt very frightened, as they lay there helpless, listening and waiting; first the sirens, then the stillness, only broken by the sound of footsteps running up the street or the voice of a mother calling to her child to hurry . . . then in the distance the ominous drone of approaching aircraft, growing louder and louder, until the heavy guns began to fire . . . like great chained watch-dogs barking at intruders . . . then the inevitable thud of bombs. You could usually tell from the sound which part of the city was under fire. Sometimes the explosion was deafening – that meant it was very close. The blast shook the house and jolted you as you lay in bed. Then you held your breath and prayed that the next one would not be a direct hit . . .

Mother would never let an air-raid upset her. She would talk on quietly, only pausing when the uproar was too loud for her voice to be heard, but that was all. Her voice didn't even tremble. 'That was pretty close,' she would comment, or 'They're bombing the docks,' or 'Remind me to give these books back to Tanya tomorrow.' So calm she seemed, while the bombs fell around them, the guns boomed, and voices in the distance shouted commands.

Boris too became gradually accustomed to the night raids. You could work yourself into a rage, if you wanted to, or tremble with fear in the dark corner of the room – you could pray or weep – but did any of these things ever do any good?

And now, while the sirens once more wailed through Leningrad – a cry of anguish wrung from the city's wounded heart – his mother acted as if nothing out of the ordinary was happening. She opened the diary, waited until it was quieter and then began to read. It was just like the times when she told him about long ago at Grandfather's house, so calm and reassuring was her voice.

'Dear diary,' she began. Boris trembled. This was Nadia's diary, and he couldn't bear it, not yet. He set his jaw and clenched his fists beneath the blankets. He took a deep breath and began to listen, and slowly his grief drifted away. Through his mother's words he began to see a new Nadia, not the Nadia who now lay dead in that cold room, but a Nadia who would always remain alive . . .

Dear diary,

Today I went out with Serjozja and we bought you

in Dimitri Smuul's shop – Dimitri always has a drip at the end of his nose, and I was so scared that it was going to fall on you! For I'm determined to keep you nice and clean, and my very own private friend . . .

Boris even smiled. All his pain disappeared. He could imagine Nadia hopping on one foot in that shop, keeping an eye all the time on Dimitri's nose . . .

If you really can keep a secret, diary, I'm going to tell you everything that happens, and all my thoughts. Am I a silly girl, diary? Sometimes I think I must be different from everyone else – or is everyone different from everyone else? After I had bought you I had to go to the canteen. We got gorgeous soup, but Father would hardly eat any of it. He gave his helping to Serjozja and me. Mother was angry. 'You must eat,' she said. But Father said he wasn't hungry. Diary dear, you don't know my father as well as I do. I know why he can't eat. He would rather I didn't know, but I do. On Monday or Tuesday (I can't remember which, but it doesn't matter anyway) Boris's father came to see us. He wanted to know if Father would go as his co-driver, with the lorries that bring supplies to the city from across Lake Ladoga. Father waited for a long time before he answered, then he said: 'I daren't, Alexei Makarenko; I will do anything else, but I just cannot drive across that well of death.'

Alexei Makarenko wasn't angry. He's such a nice man. He just laid his hand on Father's shoulder, and do you know what he said? (No, of course you don't know, for at the time you were still lying in Dimitri Smuul's shop.) He said: 'Only a brave man has the courage to admit he knows fear.' He was just about to say good-bye when he noticed me. And then he realized that it was for the sake of me and Mother and Serjozja that Father would not drive over the lake. Father is certainly not a coward, diary. He is just different from other people – a bit like me. And then, when it was time for supper, he simply refused to eat . . .

The monotonous drone of planes flying at a height came gradually nearer. The anti-aircraft guns in the lines outside the city began to fire. It wouldn't last much longer.

Boris didn't listen to these noises, horrid messengers of destruction and death. He listened only to the gentle voice of his mother . . .

Can you understand, my diary, how Father's eyes make me feel so sad? He looks so . . . so . . . I don't

know how to describe it. But you'll know how he looks. Perhaps it's because he doesn't paint any longer — and he's such a marvellous artist. Do you know that there are three of Father's paintings in the Hermitage, along with etchings and paintings by people like Rembrandt? Perhaps one day we'll go and look at them again . . .

It's getting dark now. I'll write more in the morning. How nice it is to be able to write all this to you. Oh, I quite forgot to tell you that there's a war on . . .

Guns fired on all sides. Searchlights cut the sky like great white swords. Near at hand a machine-gun began to rattle, meaning that a plane would soon nose-dive towards the city. Boris held his breath and waited. Yes, there went the first bomb.

Boris stiffened. Without meaning to, he clutched his mother, as if her slender shoulder could give him refuge. Mother stroked his hand, but she went on reading, just as though nothing unusual was happening . . .

I've laughed so much today: I've been playing on the stairs with Boris — such silly games. That's what's so nice about Boris, he never makes fun of my games and he knows nearly as many as I do. He's the only boy I know that can play quietly. All the other boys shout and yell and are so rude, but Boris never hurts anyone.

First we played 'Knock-knock!' — you jump down a step for every good answer. Then we just asked crazy questions, and they got crazier and crazier.

'Why is the sky a dirty grey today?'

'Because the sun's spent the day in bed,' answered Boris.

And that was quite true because the sun didn't come out once the whole day. We played for ages, until we were sore from laughing. Then we took round some notices for the civil defence people . . .

Now the bombs were falling much faster. The raid would be over in a few minutes – though a few minutes could seem like centuries. Mother read on, but Boris could only hear a word here and there now. The city shook – as if a violent thunderstorm had burst over the streets. Boris shut his eyes, but in his mind he could still see the bombs raining down. How many were still to drop on the battered city from the terror-filled sky? He burrowed deeper under the blankets.

Just then there was an uncanny stillness. Was the raid over? Uncertainty hung silent and threatening above the house. The raid began again . . .

Boris relaxed with a sigh. There was an ear-splitting crash and the whole house shook. The big portrait of Grandfather fell from the wall with a bang. Dishes crashed from the dresser and shattered on the floor; the knives and forks clattered in the drawer; flakes of plaster floated from the ceiling. This time Boris really clung to his mother. At last all was still again, except for distant sounds of gunfire.

'That was very close,' remarked Mother.

Cautiously Boris opened his eyes. The room was pitch dark. The candle had gone out. But the danger was past.

'Shall I go on reading?'

'No,' cried Boris, 'no more just now! Tomorrow!'

'Shall we try to sleep then?'

'Yes,' murmured Boris. He pushed the blankets aside and went over to his own bed. He felt pieces of the ceiling beneath his feet. But when he lay in his own bed, sleep refused to come. Nadia was dead, but the pain was not so bad now. Tomorrow he'd read a bit more of her diary – he'd always have that. And tomorrow too he'd find out where that last bomb had fallen . . .

'Will you tell me a story about long ago?' It was best to forget all about the present.

Mother raised herself slightly on her pillows and began to tell once again about the big house where she had lived when she was a little girl.

The all-clear sounded. Vaguely Boris heard voices in the distance. First-aid posts, emergency stations, ambulances, firemen and salvage workers would be busy tonight . . .

14

Boris sat at the table in front of the window reading Nadia's diary. Mother had a nap every afternoon, and she was still sound asleep.

It made Boris sad and yet happy to read the sentences that Nadia had written in her springy handwriting. Sometimes the writing was careless, and then very neat, usually when she had started a new page. But after a few lines the neatness would disappear. It was clear that she had trouble in keeping pace with her thoughts. It was lucky that he had known Nadia so well, for he understood all the words and what she had been thinking as she wrote them; he knew exactly what every short phrase meant . . .

Dear diary. I feel afraid. From my ankles to my hair. Only my feet are brave – they walk about everywhere as usual. Shall I tell you what a coward I've been? Today the big van came and took away Ivan's mother and little Nina, and Vera Polova as well, who had died the day before. I couldn't bear to watch. I'll have to learn how to die bravely, although I'd rather learn to live happily.

Does anyone really know why we're alive? Here in Leningrad everyone knows why we fight, feel hunger, die – for freedom. But is freedom the only thing to live for?

I'm so stupid, I don't know anything about life and a lot less about death.

I think I'd like to act in films when I grow up, and make people happy. But I don't think that could ever happen. Who would want to look at a skinny-scraggy-scarecrow like me?

It's been raining all day. Heaven's been crying, but there are no more tears in Leningrad. Everyone is so brave. It is awful that I'm such a coward . . .

Boris stared out of the window. Nadia had certainly never been a coward.

On the opposite side of the street, old Granny Olesha trudged along the path between the banks of snow. She was carrying two small jugs of frozen water. How strange that such an old person should still be alive, when Nadia, so young, had died. Boris was sure it was more than six months ago that he had heard old Granny saying to his mother: 'I've had my time, my dear. This war's like a film that I'm seeing for the second time . . .' Yet there she was still, plodding through the snow . . .

His mother muttered in her sleep. The sheets rustled as she turned restlessly. Once again Boris felt a spine-chilling fear that his mother might die. She had been very cheerful that morning, but it was plain to see she was far from well. What should he do if there was no Mother to turn to . . . ?

Granny Olesha had reached her house now. Slowly, stopping on each step, she climbed the stairs to her door. Was she asking a question for every tread? Or did she have no more questions left to ask, being so old?

Boris returned to his reading, to Nadia's hopes and fears, her courage, her worries, her laughter . . .

Dear diary, do you know the distance between life and death? Today a man was walking along in front of me. Suddenly he stopped and dropped to the ground.

I ran up to him to see if I could help him. But he was already dead. You live, you move, you think, you see, you breathe, and then suddenly – snap! It's all over. What is the very last thought a person thinks? . . . I can't decide why everything should end so suddenly. Perhaps there is a heaven where all questions are answered. If I die, perhaps I'll find out the answers. I've been thinking a lot about death recently. Father's ill – he's been in bed for the last few days. If he didn't look so dreadfully ill and sad I'd be happy, for it's nice to have him at home all day.

Boris looked over at his mother's bed. Had Nadia realized that her father was going to die? Quickly he turned over a few pages . . .

Dear diary, I'm glad I live in Leningrad. With its fine palaces and museums and theatres, and old yellow-stone houses reflected in the canals, and all the parks and squares, and the churches with their golden domes – it must be the most beautiful as well as the bravest city in all Russia. But for how much longer? Yesterday there was another heavy raid. The bombs fell very near us. My teeth were chattering with fright.

'Just listen to her teeth chattering and her knees knocking,' teased Serjozja. He was laughing to try and cheer me up.

But what's the point of being cheerful if your house collapses on top of you? The cook at the canteen lost his whole family that way. Yet there he was as usual, doling out the soup. I'm glad no one complained that day that the soup was watery.

Perhaps some day I'll be brave enough to help other people, although it makes me sad. Someone's got to try . . . Diary, shall I be a doctor one day? If 'one day' ever comes . . .

The letterbox rattled. Boris sat up in surprise. There hadn't been a post for weeks. He got up and tiptoed to the door. On the mat lay a yellow envelope. Wondering, Boris picked it up. It was addressed to his mother. In the top left-hand corner were the printed words: COMMITTEE FOR WELFARE OF CHILDREN, LENINGRAD. For heaven's

sake! Boris stood transfixed. Was this the evacuation notice? Would he have to report tomorrow or the day after? It had been freezing for days now. Were the lorries on their way over the lake again? But he was not going. He wouldn't go. Boris scratched his head and stared at the envelope. Should he hide it? Throw it away?

'Boris, what are you doing?'

'I'm just . . .' Boris couldn't think of anything to say.

'Come here a moment.'

Boris stuffed the letter into his pocket and walked slowly into the room, hoping that his mother wouldn't look at him too closely.

His mother was sitting up in bed. She peered at Boris short-sightedly.

'What was that?'

Reluctantly Boris pulled the envelope from his pocket. It seemed crazy to try to conceal it, especially as his mother was looking at him so suspiciously. He gave her the envelope.

'Well now,' said his mother. She tore open the envelope and glanced quickly over the green card that was inside it. Was that his evacuation card?

'Oh, Boris,' cried his mother. She sounded very pleased. 'It's an invitation to the theatre!'

'The theatre?' It sounded impossible. 'The theatre?' repeated Boris.

Mother nodded. 'To celebrate Christmas and New Year a play for children will be performed in the City Theatre, Leningrad.'

'When is it?' Boris didn't believe it. There was something funny about the card.

'The day after tomorrow, at three o'clock.' Mother

studied the card more closely. 'It lasts until seven. Perhaps . . .' She hesitated.

'Perhaps what?'

'Perhaps you'll get supper.'

'Why?'

'Because it doesn't finish until seven o'clock.'

Boris didn't reply. He couldn't decide what to make of this peculiar invitation. Mother had leaned back on her pillows and was examining the card again. What did it mean? Suddenly he saw the explanation quite clearly.

None of the children in Leningrad wanted to be evacuated. Was the play a trap – a bait to gather them all together? Would they be hustled out of the theatre into the waiting lorries?

A tornado of thoughts whirled in Boris's mind. The more he thought about it, the more probable it seemed. Each lorry could hold twenty children. And if there were a hundred lorries that meant two thousand children. And there were two thousand seats in the theatre. The time fitted too, because the lorries would drive through the night.

He became aware of his mother's watchful gaze.

'Don't you like the idea?'

'No,' said Boris, honestly. 'I don't think I'll bother going,' he added.

'But I want you to go. For one thing, you may get a good meal. And wouldn't it be a change to be among other children?'

Boris shook his head.

'But why not?'

Boris shrugged his shoulders. He tried to avoid his mother's eyes. Did she know what the invitation really meant? Icy fear clutched at Boris's heart again, as he shifted restlessly from one foot to the other. Mother wanted him to go. There could be only one reason for that – she knew that she was going to die, just as Vera's mother and the mothers of Ivan and Gregory had known. Did she want to die alone? Did she want to get him away before that time, so that it wouldn't be more difficult for her than it was already?

'Darling, what's the matter?'

'I'm not going,' said Boris.

'You are going,' said his Mother. 'It is very important that you get a good meal.'

'I won't.' Boris's voice grew stubborn. 'I will not go.'

'Yes, you will,' said his mother, very firmly indeed. Slowly Boris walked over to the table where Nadia's diary lay. If Nadia were still alive what would she have told him to do? Hide? But it was too cold to hide anywhere for long. Plead with his mother? But what if she really felt she had to be alone . . . ?

'Boris.'

Boris looked at his mother. The worry and care had gone from her eyes. She smiled, as if she understood everything.

'You don't want to go because of Nadia, is that it? I can understand that very well.' She spoke gently, without looking at him. 'Shall I read you a bit more from her diary?'

Boris bit his lip. Now his mother was sure to think that he didn't want to go to the play without Nadia. He felt ashamed that for the moment he hadn't even thought of that.

He picked up the diary and took it to his mother. Confused thoughts and feelings tumbled through him as he went and sat by her side. Would they soon come to the last page? Would it be very sad? A heavy lorry rumbled down the street – loaded with snow, with rubble or with water? Or was it the big van . . . ?

His mother began to read softly.

Dusk crept slowly into the room. Would they get to the end before it was dark?

As Boris listened he became a part again of the innocent, wise world of Nadia Morozova. She had written so lovingly of her father, her mother and Serjozja, of the people in the streets, even of the war.

Once or twice Boris felt a lump in his throat and he had some trouble blinking back his tears. More often he smiled as Nadia's vivid words spilled out over the page. She wrote just as she talked . . .

About the fortifications round the city:

'At first it was as if Leningrad had tied an apron round herself to keep herself clean – but now it's a butcher's apron splattered with blood . . .'

About her diary:

'You are like a looking-glass, where I can see myself and everyone I love – but something's cracked you, and I don't know if you can be mended . . .'

About Boris:

'He understands so well – we don't have to tell each other what we're thinking . . .'

One thing stood out more clearly than all the others: how much Nadia had found to love in the world. She could forgive anyone anything. 'Why not – surely no one has made himself what he is.'

Mother read on and on, page after page. Sometimes there were blots and smudges. Nadia always made pictures out of them. It was so like her to be able to get fun out of ink-blots – an elephant . . . a gnome with a long beard . . . flowers and stars and snowflakes . . . dogs and cats . . .

It grew darker and darker in the room. Now his mother was reading the last few pages . . .

Oh, diary. Today my father died. I knew it had to happen, but not that it would be so soon. Father and Serjozja were still asleep this morning (Serjozja has pneumonia and he is very ill) so Mother and I were going about on tiptoe. Suddenly Father called me. 'Nadia!'

I went over to him. He took my hand and smiled at me, and his dear eyes were no longer sad. He looked at me for a long time.

'Live long enough to know that life is a joy,' he said, so quietly I could barely hear him. Then he shut his eyes, sighed and gave a little nod. His hand slid from mine, and he died before Mother could come over to the bed.

Oh, diary, he was the best father in all the world.

His mother turned the page and Boris saw that she had come to the last one. In the middle of the page the writing tailed off in a scrawl . . .

Diary, diary, diary, I must talk to you.

This morning Serjozja didn't wake up . . . Last night, neither of us could sleep, and he told me where I could find some food. I want to talk to you, diary, but words are so difficult to find . . .

That was the day we went to the canteen, thought Boris. Together they had made the long journey into No-man's-land. Nadia hadn't had enough strength left to describe it. It wasn't difficult to imagine what had happened the last day. Boris could see Nadia vividly, as she sat writing at the table.

Dear diary, I've only got you now. Mother died during the night and I didn't even know . . . I'm on my own now . . . too tired to tell you any more. It's snowing outside. Leningrad must now fight in a torn white cloak. I know why . . . freedom only comes when everyone is happy.

It is not difficult to die, but it was marvellous to be alive. Will something just go 'snap' inside me?

It's growing lighter and lighter . . . I think I can see a path through the snowflakes, millions of snow-flakes, whirling and dancing . . . they seem to have faces . . .

Father, Mother, Serjozja . . .

Diary . . . I'm not afraid any more . . . I wish I could . . .

Mother's voice stopped. They were quiet for a long time in the twilight. Later, much later, after he had been a long time in bed, Boris remembered the card that had come. Should he go? What would Nadia have said if she had still been alive? Nadia was dead, but Boris had the comforting feeling that she was still very near to him . . .

15

'Yes, you are going,' repeated his mother. She sounded quite decided. With a hopeless, helpless feeling, Boris looked at the clock on the dresser. It was two o'clock. The play was due to begin in an hour, and he would have to leave in fifteen minutes.

'You must go,' said his mother again. 'You can't lose the chance of getting a good meal.'

'Who says we'll get anything to eat?'

'I think you will,' Mother replied. 'Uncle Vanya will be doing everything possible to see that you do.'

'I don't care – I'm not going,' declared Boris obstinately. He tried not to look at his mother. If he saw tears in her eyes he'd have to give in, he knew that for certain.

This was the third time they'd argued about the theatre. Boris was determined to resist to the uttermost, because going to the theatre would mean saying good-bye, good-bye to his mother, good-bye to Leningrad. Surely the more sorrow, the more fear, the more uncertainty there was, the more necessary it was to stay beside each other? That must be a comfort right to the very end. Hadn't Nadia written so in her diary?

But Mother understood nothing of that. Mother wanted him to go and live safely in far-off Sverdlovsk, with Olga Petrovna. But he wasn't going.

'Silly boy. You really won't be sorry if you go.'

Mother's voice was gently imploring. When she spoke like that it was difficult to go against her wishes and make her unhappy.

'But what about you if I go?'

'I'll be able to enjoy my afternoon rest in peace and quiet.'

Boris looked doubtfully at his mother. How white and helpless she looked! Once again he felt convinced that she wanted to get him out of the way, that she thought time was short; that she wanted to be alone to die.

'Come here a minute.'

There was no escape. Slowly Boris walked over to her bed.

'Here is the card. Don't lose it. Put it in your pocket.' Boris took the card.

'And take the lamp with you. It will be dark by the time you come out.'

Boris nodded. The way Mother was looking at him so pleadingly made any more resistance impossible. He went to the dresser to fetch the bicycle lamp. Listlessly, he turned the knob once or twice, until a feeble beam shone out.

Should he go? Or should he just pretend he was going? He could go and watch outside the theatre to see what happened and then come back home after it was all over.

Boris pulled on his fur cap. He touched Father's revolver in his coat pocket. Slowly he walked back to the bed, but he just couldn't look at his mother's face again. He gave her a kiss.

'Good-bye, Mother.'

'Good-bye, dear. I hope you have a lovely time.'

Did she mean that she hoped he would have a lovely time at Olga Petrovna's? Was this good-bye for ever?

Boris didn't dare look to see if his mother was now fighting back her tears. If this really was a parting, for ever, he was sure he would be able to read it in her face. But he wouldn't, and couldn't, look at her. Reluctantly he went out.

Nadia would have said that the sky had a dirty face today, thought Boris. He trailed along the narrow path between the banks of snow towards the theatre. An icy wind from the Neva blew through the city. In the distance the spires of the cathedral of St. Peter and St. Paul, on its island in the Neva, stood out above the roof-tops. There lay buried the tsars and tsarinas of the Russia of long ago. Entombed in fine marble for centuries: Peter the Great, Elizabeth, Catherine the Great, the Pauls and the Alexanders. But he would never know where Nadia lay buried. Boris shuddered at the thought of the mass graves that had had to be dug behind the new part of the city. He turned the corner, walked along a narrow street, crossed a square, and then began to walk, slower and slower, by a canal leading to the centre of the town.

Was he going to go to the theatre, or would he hang about until it was seven o'clock and he could go back home?

Despair and doubt black as the clouds above him swept through Boris. From the houses the past gazed down on him. Had Peter the Great walked up and down here, when he had commanded the building of Leningrad on the marshy ground? Tens of thousands of slaves, serfs and prisoners-of-war had laboured – with their bare hands when necessary – to lay the foundations. Here the tsars and tsarinas had had their marvellous palaces built. Their almost incredible richness still dazzled one's eyes in many parts of the city. How much sorrow had these old buildings witnessed? Here, amidst the palaces, beggars had shuffled through the streets, some with children that they hired for a few kopeks and stripped to the skin so as to rouse compassion in passers-by. Here thousands of mothers had left their babies as foundlings, because they couldn't feed them. Here at one time a girl of noble birth had burned herself alive, hoping that by her sacrifice the world would admit that it was filled with injustice.

It was in Leningrad that the great Revolution had broken out, with the ideal of bringing all injustice to an end. But had the hoped-for better world been achieved?

Boris's thoughts turned to Nadia and the words she had written in her diary: 'Freedom only comes when everyone is happy.' Was it for freedom that two hundred thousand men and women of Leningrad had volunteered to serve among the soldiers of the Red Army and the sailors in the fleet? And what about the Germans who had saved Nadia and himself? Were they fighting for freedom? Boris's thoughts returned to his mother. What chance had she to live in happiness? He would do anything in the world for her except go to Sverdlovsk.

More and more slowly Boris plodded through the snow. He felt cold and ... hungry.

Boris stood across the street from the theatre. He saw a stream of children going in the main entrance. Some had been brought by their mothers, but mostly they were alone. A friendly looking lady with an arm-band was ushering them in. In a long crocodile marched the children from the orphanage, in charge of prefects, who, rather like sheep-dogs, were having a bit of trouble keeping their lambs in order. Among them Boris saw Ivan, walking hand in hand with a little girl. Ivan's hat was at least

three times too big for him. Boris would have liked to ask
him about the orphanage, but he thought he'd better not.
The orphans disappeared inside. Were they all evacuees
too? Would they all have to drive over Lake Ladoga?
What if Ivan were drowned . . . and the others?

After a while Boris began to get restless. He looked at
the children going in laughing and unconcerned. He
watched carefully to see what sort of good-byes the
mothers were saying to their sons and daughters. From
the distance it didn't look as though they were never going
to see each other again. Would they really be going back
home again after the play – or after supper?

Boris's mouth began to water. He could forget the cold,
but he couldn't stop thinking about food. Should he go in?

Cautiously he crossed the street and stood close to the entrance. Could he smell soup? An old woman who was clearing away the snow leaned on her broom and smiled at him.

'Aren't you going inside?'

Boris was at a loss for words. The lady with the arm-band came up just then.

'Have you a card?'

'Are we going to get something to eat?'

'Have you a card?'

Boris hesitated for a moment longer. For the last time he weighed the chance of food against the chance of evacuation. Then he pulled out the card and showed it to the lady.

'Come on in then, dreamy.'

He felt a gentle hand on his shoulder pushing him inside.

Boris was given a seat right in the middle. Some of the big lights were burning. He didn't know how that was possible. Next to him was a girl who looked as though she'd put on her best dress for the outing. He could see a bit of red material under her coat. 'That was nice of her – she didn't have to dress up,' thought Boris. It was very cold – they had all kept their coats on. He felt sorry for the girl, for no one could see what a pretty dress she was wearing, but he didn't like to tell her that he liked it.

On his other side was a boy with a fur cap just like Boris's. He stared straight ahead of him, gloomy and silent. There didn't seem to be anybody to talk to. Boris looked round to see if he could see Ivan anywhere. But there were so many children. So many furry hats . . .

Were they going to get something to eat? Boris could

smell nothing. Behind him were two giggling girls. As Boris looked round he saw one of them, a fair-haired girl with brown eyes, stretch out her hand and jerk off his neighbour's hat.

'Give me that!' The boy jumped up; Boris saw that his hair had been cut off close to his scalp and that he had some sort of rash on his head. No wonder he was angry! The girls in the row behind began to pass the hat along the row, but the boy made a grab for it. A fight began. The girls giggled. Another lady with an arm-band came rushing up and dragged the boy away. She led him outside, without his hat. Would he get nothing to eat now?

Boris stared at the girls. They were still sitting giggling. He could have slapped their faces, the stupid kids. But just then the lights dimmed and the curtains slowly parted. On the stage – a handsome room of pre-Revolutionary times. Paper flowers on the window-sill, and through the glass you could see a blue sky, with the sun shining. But in the fine sunny room the actors sat and moved in their winter clothes. 'It must be cold on the stage too,' Boris thought. He realized that the actors couldn't be expected to act in summer clothes, but their thick coats made it all less real. He tried to concentrate on the play, but he didn't succeed. The girl next to him was biting her nails. In front of him a little boy whispered to his big brother: 'Are we going to eat soon?'

On the stage the actors and actresses were doing their best. The audience of children watched them, but most of them didn't understand why the people in the play were making such a fuss about nothing. The hero of the play wasn't very heroic, compared with the young men of Leningrad. The girl who was defying her wicked uncle was scarcely a heroine, when you remembered the women who had dug out huge blocks of ice and dragged them into the roads to obstruct the German advance – and did it while bombs and shells exploded around them. And what did it matter that the girl in the play, wrapped in her warm coat, was ill, when in the reality outside hundreds were dying of hunger.

Boris sat hunched in his seat. He tried to enjoy the play, but his thoughts kept wandering. To Mother; to Uncle Vanya, who wanted to save all the children; to the German officer, who had risked his life to save Nadia's, and yet Nadia had had only two days longer to live . . .

Nadia! If she had been sitting next to him, how they would have made jokes about the actors in their thick coats. Then the least thing would have been something to laugh at.

The actors babbled on, but Boris was now lost in his own thoughts. He thought about the war, about the brave partisans who fought behind the German lines, about the evacuation. He thought again about the meals that he had sometimes refused to eat before the war, and then suddenly, for no reason, he thought of Peter the Great, whose statue, now covered with sand-bags, stood in front of the Admiralty. If Peter the Great were alive now, he would be grieved to see his fine city almost in ashes.

From time to time Boris looked at the faces of the children around him. He became aware of the suspense in the hall. But it wasn't caused by the play or the actors. One question was clearly written on the doubtful, hopeful, tense face of every child there:

'Will there be something to eat when it's over?'

16

When the curtain fell, most of the children forgot to clap. Although the cast had done their best, they hadn't been able to compete against such hunger, such intense longing for food. Every child in the auditorium was on his feet as soon as the play was over. Eagerly they craned their necks. Were they going to get something to eat or not? Rumours about food had been going round so often during the performance that there had to be some truth in them.

'Sit still, please sit still,' called a lady with an arm-band.

But no one paid the slightest attention. Some children were punching each other, partly in fun but more in an attempt to keep warm. Others were stamping their feet on the floor.

Suddenly Boris caught sight of Uncle Vanya. He was standing at the back of the hall talking to a group of children, who soon began to laugh and look very cheerful.

'Uncle Vanya! Uncle Vanya!' Boris shouted as loud as he could, but Uncle Vanya didn't hear him.

'Sit still, you must wait your turn.' The first few rows were led out.

'Are we going to eat?' asked one girl.

'Sit down. Keep in your places!'

It seemed ages, but at last it was time for Boris's row. Meekly they walked behind another lady with an arm-band. Boris saw that all their faces were as expectant as his own. What was it to be? A mug of soup? A slice of bread? A bar of chocolate . . .

They were taken into another hall. A quiver of delight ran through the whole row. Long tables stood ready laid with knives and forks and spoons. Candles were burning. Piles of soup plates and huge urns stood at one side. A buzz of excited talk broke out from the children.

'Supper! We're going to get a real supper!'

They were told to go forward. 'Gently! Take your time. There's room for everyone.'

Boris stood still for a moment. What a marvellous sight – the tables all laid, the candles, the smiling faces of the children; they were dancing with excitement, scarcely daring to believe the treat possible . . . with wide, anxious eyes they stared at the tables as they pushed towards them.

Boris found himself sitting between the girl with the pretty red dress under her furry coat, and a boy who seemed a bit older than himself. All round him whispered voices were still inquiring:

'What are we going to get?'

'Soup, anyway.'

'Beetroot soup . . .'

'Surely not – it's Christmas, after all!'

At a table farther up, they had already begun to eat. Everyone tried hard to see what they had been given . . .

Now women were coming to their table carrying big, steaming pots. They ladled out soup. And it wasn't beetroot soup; it was broth, with all sorts of vegetables and even pieces of meat in it. 'I wonder if I'll get a big plateful,' thought Boris. The boy next to him had had bad luck. His soup didn't quite come up to the rim of the plate. But Boris got a brimming ladleful. His neighbour looked at it enviously. Then he began to eat very fast, without taking his eyes off his plate – with his arm round it, as if someone might come and take it away again.

On the opposite side of the table two girls murmured
grace and made the sign of the cross. They might well do
so, for it was good soup. Boris, too, said a prayer of thanks
for his full plate, although he was a bit doubtful if God
would hear it, for no doubt he had lots of more important
prayers to listen to because of the war. Boris began to eat,
slowly and carefully, trying to make each spoonful last as
long as possible.

It really was lovely soup. Nice and warm, and you
could taste the meat in it. At the third mouthful Boris
remembered his mother. How right she had been to insist
that he should come. Not a word had been said about

evacuation or lorries. Had he got himself all worked up for nothing? And had he just imagined that his mother wanted to die without him there? Perhaps she wasn't going to die after all. Boris felt quite carefree as he realized that he had imagined all sorts of nasty things that might never happen.

More cheerful than he had felt for ages, Boris turned his attention to his soup again and raised his spoon . . .

'We're going to get something else,' said the boy next to him, when the women were taking away their empty plates.

'Yes, I think we are,' replied Boris. Everyone had swallowed their soup in silence, but now, with some food inside them, they began to talk. The hot soup had made them feel much more friendly. Should Boris tell the boy next to him about their adventures in No-man's-land? But the boy forestalled him.

'My brother's fighting with the partisans,' he informed him.

'He must be terribly brave,' said Boris, impressed. He had heard a lot about the partisans. Little groups of them lived in the woods, right among the German lines. They crept out of their hiding-places to destroy roads, blow up bridges, set fire to German camps, and altogether do as much damage as possible.

'He's as brave as a lion and afraid of no one in the world,' declared the boy proudly. 'Some day I'm going to be a partisan too.'

'Perhaps when we're grown up the war will be over,' said Boris.

'I hope not!' The boy turned to Boris in horror. 'Some day my brother and I . . .'

But what he and his brother would one day do, Boris never knew. For the bread was passed round. Everyone was given two pieces. Then plates of meat and potatoes appeared.

The place was absolutely still. In utter amazement the children gazed at the slice of meat and the two potatoes on their plates. Then they furtively glanced to right and left to see if everyone was getting fair shares.

In the distance Boris could still hear the sound of guns. There were a few rifle shots. What if there were an attack now?

'Go ahead and eat. Don't just sit there watching the others.' A lady with an arm-band nudged him gently on the shoulder. Hastily Boris bent over his plate. But just as he put his knife in the meat, he remembered his mother. He could take home the bread and meat for her. In an instant he had unfolded his paper napkin and laid it on his knees. Carefully he peered around, to see if anyone was watching him. Then he picked up the meat and slipped it on to the paper. The bread followed.

Had anyone noticed? The girl across the table looked at him curiously. Boris felt his colour rising. Quickly he wrapped up the food and stuffed the package into his coat pocket, next to his father's revolver. He glanced carelessly at the girl opposite, and was relieved to see she wasn't paying any attention to him. She too seemed to be doing something beneath the table – and the half-eaten piece of meat on her plate had vanished.

Hastily Boris picked up his knife and fork and began on his potatoes. It was fine to have bread and meat in his pocket for Mother. The food would make her feel better, he was sure of that. And if only his mother went on living and got stronger he wouldn't have to go and live with Olga Petrovna in Sverdlovsk. Surely such a miracle might still happen?

17

When they had all finished eating, Uncle Vanya made a short speech.

'Dreadful things are happening, because there is a war on,' he had said. 'Leningrad has now withstood the German attack for five hundred days. But we have survived and we shall go on surviving – for our courage is unending: the courage of our soldiers, of our men and women, and also the courage of our children. We are fighting for freedom, for Russia and for a better world. Whatever may happen, do not lose that courage. Never! For then the Germans will never take this dear city of ours, no, not if they besiege it for a thousand days longer.'

After Uncle Vanya had spoken, the ladies with the armbands showed them out. Because there was no one else to thank, Boris thanked the ladies for the wonderful afternoon. Outside, some mothers were waiting in the snow, chattering with cold, but most of the children went home alone.

Boris walked part of the way with the boy who wanted to be a partisan. It was dark and bitterly cold. The snow crunched under their boots. When they came to the corner where the boy had to turn off, he asked: 'Won't you walk round this way with me?'

'No,' said Boris shortly. He was anxious to get home with his bread and meat.

'Come on, it's so dark,' pleaded the other boy, sounding very nervous.

'No, really, I can't,' said Boris.

As Boris watched him disappear in the direction of the church of St. Nicholas-of-the-Seas, he thought how queer it was that a would-be partisan should be afraid of the dark! Fear lurked everywhere . . .

The icy-cold north wind blew through the foggy streets. In the distance the heavy guns boomed ceaselessly. Was there heavy fighting going on? To hear that far-away sound made one forget one's own fear.

On Nevskiy Prospekt, the wide main street, there were still people about. But the farther Boris went from the centre of the town, the more deserted and more mysterious the streets and squares became. He began to quicken his steps, twisting the knob of the bicycle lamp until its feeble beam shone out on the path between the snow. From time to time he felt in his pocket to see if the package was still there.

The snow-decked palaces of the past looked down on him. They stood in the freezing cold night and dreamed over their tumultuous history. Their time-worn gables did not seem to be concerned with the present or the future. Shivering, Boris looked at the former palace of Prince Yussupoff, where the terrible monk Rasputin was assassinated by poison and gun-shot, for the sake of the people; behind that door was hidden the secret of his murder during a night of December 1916, when the last tsar was still reigning over Russia.

Here and there the dreary, windowless wrecks of houses stood out like scarecrows – 'the tears in Leningrad's white cloak'. In some places dark shadows flitted through the snow. With an effort, Boris tried to think of something cheerful. He'd soon be home with his precious food. And after Mother had eaten the bread and the meat, he'd tell her all about the afternoon. But the buildings seemed to be whispering their legends to him; it was as if the mighty Peter the Great, bursting with passion, shook his fist at the ruins; as if Pushkin, the great writer of the last century, had come down from his pedestal and was pacing beside the canal, seeking inspiration . . . Boris clutched the gun in his pocket tightly. Each street corner held a threat. Would someone jump out and seize the bread and meat? Would someone, mad with hunger, attack him?

Boris walked on even faster. He had still about half-an-hour's journey to go . . .

Houses, rubble, look-out posts with guns at the ready, shadows in the snow, roars of heavy cannon outside the city . . . and not far from him, perhaps only a couple of streets away, unexploded bombs – but none of these was the cause of Boris's terror. Every day you heard explosions hundreds of times. The 750,000 German soldiers surrounding the city worried him even less. You could just put up with them, and all their guns and grenades and tanks and aeroplanes. It was not the terrors of the war that gave rise to Boris's fear – no, the cause of that was one small slice of meat. He began to imagine eyes peering at him from the derelict houses, and the package in his pocket seemed to shine through his clothes . . .

Half-filled craters . . . wrecked trams still lying useless on the rails . . . a statue fallen on its side . . . a roped-off street . . . a notice-board giving warning of an unexploded bomb . . . burned-out dwellings . . . snow-covered, abandoned cars . . . a column of tanks on its way to the front . . .

The meat! Yet again Boris's hand slipped towards his pocket to feel if the packet was still there. Then he felt his father's revolver. That gave him some comfort. But the fear kept coming back. The dark, battered city was full of hidden dangers. Would that man, leaning against a wall, stop him? Was something moving among that pile of ruins? Was someone waiting his chance? Boris pulled out the gun. He let the beam of the lamp shine on it, so that everyone could see he was armed, and walked on firmly. 'It is not a crime to be afraid.' He thought of his own brave father, of Nadia, of the Germans who had saved them, even of the boy who wanted to be a partisan. But it didn't help. He felt as if something was gripping him round the throat. Every moment he expected someone to jump out at him. Then he thought he heard someone following him, cautiously, as though trying to creep up behind him . . .

A few streets farther on, a fire-engine's siren screamed through the fog. The roar of guns grew more intense, came closer, as the Russians also opened fire. The soldiers in the forward lines would be ready to receive the German fire now, to retaliate with bombs and grenades, to fight to protect Leningrad . . . A hastily blacked-out light . . . a shattered house-front . . . an old woman pulling a sledge through the snow . . . what was she pulling? . . . Barbed wire, endless barbed wire.

Footsteps! Behind him! With a start Boris realized that this time he really was being followed.

'Dear God, don't let anyone come and take away my meat,' he prayed, his fear growing stronger every moment.

Footsteps! Heavy footsteps! What was going to happen? Boris began to hurry, but the footsteps kept following. As if his life depended on it, Boris gripped the lamp and

shone its trembling beam on the revolver. He didn't dare to look round.

'Hey there, lad!'

Boris was tempted to make a run for it. But all the suspense had been too much for him and he simply couldn't make the effort. It couldn't be worse to face the enemy. He stopped. The footsteps came closer. Slowly Boris raised his eyes . . .

For a moment Boris thought it was his friend the German officer. But it was a Red Army captain. Big and solid he stood there, the snow lying thick on his fur cap.

'How do I get to Smolny, young fellow?'

Boris breathed a sigh of relief. His fear crept away among the bombed-out houses.

'Smolny?' Boris hadn't quite recovered.

'Headquarters,' explained the captain. His breath made a white trail in the fog.

What a strange question! The whole of Leningrad knew where the headquarters was.

Boris looked about him. Sometimes it was difficult to make out exactly where you were, with so many places in ruins. Quite a few streets were unrecognizable.

'You must go straight along here, until you come to the Ligovsky Prospekt. Then turn left towards the Tauride Palace . . . then past the Suvorov Museum, turn right . . . and you come to it.'

The captain shook his head with a smile. 'All these names don't mean anything to me. I've only been in the city a few days.'

'Are you a partisan?' Sometimes they even got through the German lines, Boris knew. By secret paths through the woods they brought food and medical supplies to the city, mostly stuff taken from German stores.

'No,' said the captain. 'I've come from overseas.'

He came from another world, thought Boris. Perhaps from farther away than Sverdlovsk, from where there was no war – no ruins, no blackened villages, no flattened towns and no air-raids. Would the captain know if re-inforcements were coming? Would he be able to tell him how much longer the war was going to last? A captain who was looking for the headquarters at Smolny must certainly be a very important man. 'If you like to walk with me, I'll show you the road. I have to go that way anyway.'

'That's fine,' said the captain. Then he pointed at the revolver, still clutched in Boris's hand. 'What are you doing with that?'

'Oh, hum . . . I just had it with me.' Quickly he shoved

the gun back into his pocket next to the meat, which by this time was quite frozen.

'Shall we go on then, my young friend?'

Boris nodded. He was safe now. No one would come near a captain of the Red Army. He turned round. The street behind them lay dark and empty.

'How long do you think the war will last?' Boris asked after a long silence. It must have been a very difficult question, for the captain came to a halt. He shook his head and looked about him, as if he might see the answer written in the sky.

'That I don't know, lad.'

'Will they come soon to free us?'

The captain was silent. 'Surely he doesn't think I'm afraid,' thought Boris. Quickly, he announced: 'I don't want to be evacuated, you see.'

The captain smiled and he looked even more like the German officer.

'Perhaps it would be better for you if you were, my lad. The siege might go on for a long time yet.'

'Why? Surely a miracle could happen one day.'

'Leningrad is not the only place where there's fighting. There is so much to do.'

Boris didn't need to be told that. He had often enough heard talk of the fighting in Moscow and Stalingrad, in the Ukraine, and beyond Russia, in Europe. Everyone was involved in the war; in factories, in armies, air-forces, navies. But who was involved in peace . . . when would that come, and how? No one knew the answer yet.

They came to a cross-roads. 'I go to the right here. You go straight on. Farther on there are look-out posts, and you can ask the way to Smolny.'

'Thanks a lot,' said the captain. He bent and peered into Boris's face. 'No one knows what lies ahead. But a day will come when the guns will be silent. Then we shall re-build Leningrad; brick by brick, house by house. Never forget that, my young friend. It will help you, if you keep that aim in mind . . .'

In the distance, the German guns burst out again. Bomb after bomb, shell after shell dropped on the factories on the other side of the Neva. The destruction went on, house after house, brick after brick, man after man.

With the hard-frozen slice of meat firmly clutched in his hand, Boris now entered the last stretch of the way home. There might just be enough wood left to light the stove and heat the meat for his mother . . .

18

'Is that you, Boris?'

'Yes!' called Boris. He laid his mittens on the table in the hall and went into the room. It was dark and cold. He shone the bicycle lamp on the bed. Mother screwed up her eyes against the sudden light.

'You're late!'

'I met an army captain who had to go to Smolny, and he didn't know the way, so I showed him.'

'Did you get anything to eat?'

'Yes, it was marvellous.'

'What did you have?'

'Soup and bread . . . and two potatoes,' answered Boris. He wouldn't mention the meat yet. That was to be a surprise.

'And the play – was it good?'

Boris had to think for a minute. He could hardly remember anything about it. The pretty girl, the wicked uncle, the lazy servant – they were worlds away, and what a fuss they had made about nothing at all.

'There was nothing much to it!' But, thought Boris, he'd remember all his life the hall full of children muffled in coats and caps, wondering all through the performance if they were going to get something to eat at the end. And that dream-like walk back with the ghosts of the past beckoning to him, that would always be with him too. At least he had got the bread and meat safely home. He was looking forward so much to what was about to happen.

'Now, you must turn your back to the room, Mother. Don't look over here until I tell you.'

'Why not?' She was looking at him in wonder.

'I've got a surprise for you.'

'What *have* you been up to?' She began to get curious.

'Just shut your eyes and don't look,' insisted Boris; but his mother still hesitated.

Even in the dim torchlight, it looked as if his mother had answered the question herself; as if she might refuse the treat that Boris had in store for her.

'She'd better not say that she's not hungry,' he thought. Everyone was hungry. They got four ounces of bread a day, except those who did heavy work and they got double rations. Even so, in the factories they sometimes collapsed behind their machines. Mother needn't bother to say that she wasn't hungry, as she probably would to save the meat for him.

They looked at each other. It was as if his mother could see through him; as if she could see the packet of food tucked in his pocket. At last she smiled. 'Well, I'm curious!' And she turned over on her side.

Boris tiptoed over to the stove in the corner. He crushed an old newspaper into a ball and covered it with the last sticks of fire-wood from the basket. He struck a match . . . Then he got the small saucepan out of the kitchen dresser. It was right at the back of the cupboard, with a lot of other things in front of it, because it hadn't been used for months. Holding it close to the bicycle lamp, he wiped the pan clean with a piece of newspaper. The sticks began to crackle. Boris held out his cold hands to the flames, which looked like tiny dancers among the cinders. Then he carefully put the pan on the fire.

The paper had frozen to the piece of meat, so Boris put the whole package in the pan. When it began to melt he would be able to unwrap the bread and the meat. He set a plate ready, with a knife and fork, and a glass of water out of the big jug – and that wasn't at all simple, for there was a thick layer of ice on top, which he had to smash before he could get at the water.

Outside, the guns still boomed. Outside, lay the imprisoned city. Outside, Leningrad fought her stubborn, bitter fight for freedom – a fight that had now lasted for five hundred days. But Boris had quite forgotten the world outside this little room. On the tiny fire he heated the slice of meat for his mother. He had to take very good care of it, in case the food burnt.

The meat was much, much more than just a piece of meat. To Boris it was a kind of magic medicine, which would cure his mother and make her strong again, so that he wouldn't have to be sent away. All his heart and mind was concentrated on that small meal. The sticks sparked. The meat in the pan began to sizzle and a lovely smell of cooking food filled the room. Boris felt very grateful and very happy . . .

It was all ready. He had pulled the table up to the bed and placed the bicycle lamp on it, and the plate and the glass were neatly arranged.

Mother was still lying with her face to the wall. She didn't move. She couldn't have helped hearing sounds and smelling the food, but not a word had she said.

Boris felt the meat with his finger; it was nice and hot, so he put it on the plate. Slowly he walked over to the bed. They were the happiest steps he had ever taken in his life. After Mother had eaten, everything would be different.

Life would be worth living again. Should he light the candle, so that it would be just like a real party? He lit it. Boris gave a last look at the feast: a plate with bread and a slice of meat – in the light of a candle-stump.

'Mother!' He could have shouted with joy. 'Mother! You can look now . . .'

His mother turned over, quickly wiping her face with a corner of the sheet. In the flickering light of the candle, Boris could see that she had been crying.

His mother sat up and looked . . . for a moment there was silence. There are times when mothers simply must not cry. She bit her lips and gripped the blankets hard. She tried to speak, but couldn't. She screwed up her eyes, as if she couldn't believe what she saw.

'It's for you,' said Boris triumphantly.

'Oh Boris . . . Boris dear!' said his mother. Then: 'Oh, Boris dear . . .'

'Don't let it get cold!' said Boris, putting the fork into her hand. At last his mother managed to speak. For a moment she looked about to argue. But Boris had a wise mother. She knew that in this life there are some gifts which cannot be refused.

'Darling, what a wonderful surprise,' she said, smiling through her tears. 'I just can't help crying, I'm so happy.'

For a mother who never thought of herself, it must have been a tremendous effort to draw that plate towards her. But she cut the meat and began to eat, with tiny little bites. She ate very slowly, as if she had trouble swallowing, thought Boris. Of course, she would eat it like that because the food was so delicious and she wanted to make it last as long as possible . . .

19

It was midnight and the sound of gunfire seemed to echo to the very stars. But tonight Boris was not living through a nightmare. They had talked for a long time and then Mother had fallen into a deep, peaceful sleep. Boris could hear her calm breathing whenever the guns were silent for a few minutes. But he himself couldn't get to sleep. He lay and waited for a miracle. From the moment he had arrived home the feeling had grown inside him that everything was going to be different from now on. It had to be, even if the slice of meat hadn't any magical powers. It didn't matter – something was bound to happen. Perhaps it had already happened.

'I have changed,' thought Boris. It had happened since the theatre, when he had walked home through the charred streets; in terror, in grief, in despair. Then, as he had been carrying the plate of food across to his mother, he had suddenly felt quite certain that life was going to be happier from then on. At last he had understood quite clearly what Nadia's father had meant. Nadia! All at once the memory of her came back to him. Although she was dead and he would never see her again, so much of her still belonged to him; just like his own father, she would never really die; her smile, her thoughts, her dreams – these he would never forget . . .

With sudden certainty Boris knew too that the battered city itself would never die; whatever was destroyed, whoever was killed, something would still remain — the spirit of the workers who died at their machines, the spirit of the women who penetrated into No-man's-land at the risk of their lives to fell trees and drag back sledge-loads of wood to the frozen city. They didn't just bring warmth to the stoves — by their courage, they lit fires in people's hearts. As if the whole world had suddenly been filled with light, Boris understood now why Nadia wanted 'to take all the brave people in the world in her arms'.

A thousand thoughts whirled in Boris's mind as he lay with closed eyes beneath the blankets. But this time they were happy thoughts; care and fear and sorrow had faded for ever.

He had talked for ages with his mother that night. He had confessed what he had never dared to mention before — he had told her about his dread of crossing the ice in the lorries, to die as his father had done; then they had talked about Nadia. After that it was not difficult to make Mother understand that there was no need for him to be sent away. Now he no longer sulked like a troublesome child, but reasoned like a man.

'I shall stay in Leningrad, so that I can look after you.'

Mother had thought for a bit, but not for long.

'Perhaps you're right, Boris. We shall see what Uncle Vanya says in the morning.'

So they would stay together. That was right, for in war everyone had need of each other. Only if they stood together in hope and faith could they survive the horror of war.

Cannons, bombs, mortars and machine-guns, they were all going mad together. Boris's thoughts turned to the German officer. Was he now lying behind his machine-gun in the snow, fighting for his life? Why couldn't all Russians and all Germans throw away their weapons and make friends? Wouldn't that be easier than all this fighting?

'I have changed,' thought Boris again, for he felt no hate any more and he could think about peace. Less than a week ago, he had, like everyone else in Leningrad, been eaten up with bitter hatred for the Germans. That very hate had helped him to swallow back his tears and had supported him through all that had to be endured – the air-raids, the flames, the corpses in the snow. 'I'll kill them, all of them. They must be wiped out.' Words like these got you past the worst times. But could you build a new city with them? The encounter in No-man's-land had taught Boris that not all Germans were bad. The German officer was a friend. He had saved Nadia's life, although that life was only to last for two days longer. And during those last two days Nadia had written those pages in her diary, those words that would never die . . .

Was that the miracle: that hate was conquered by war? Or was the miracle that Leningrad could not be conquered, though every house in every street lay in ruins?

'We shall build the city again,' the captain had assured him, 'brick by brick.' When you looked at the rubble it didn't seem possible, but if you remembered the spirit of the people, then it was a miracle that could well happen.

'To know that life is a joy.' Now Boris knew exactly what Nadia's father's last words meant.

And so his own private miracle really had happened; he had changed. From the moment he had seen that great German boot standing next to him in the snow the change had begun in him. Only, he hadn't noticed it. The enemy had been transformed and was a friend. For all his living days Boris would remember that German officer . . .

The cannons blasted on. The worst bombardment seemed to be to the south of the city. A thousand bombs and shells might plunge to earth before the attack was over.

'These things happen,' Mother had often said. But did they have to happen? Out of the chaos, kind deeds and gentle voices shone like stars . . . That was how all people should act, how all voices should speak . . .

Boris thought now of all the men in the fighting lines, the Germans and the Russians. 'Please God, let the war end. Let us all be free and happy.'

All through the darkness of that night Leningrad shuddered unceasingly. The terrible battering went on until dawn. In the icy room the knives and forks rattled in the dresser drawer. But Boris slept and, as he slept, he smiled . . .

20

Boris did not waken until the front-door slammed and footsteps rushed along the passage. Uncle Vanya burst into the room. The beam on his face was as broad as the Neva.

'We've made a break through the German lines,' he exclaimed. 'We've got control of the railway. Last night we made contact with free Russia. The first trains with supplies are on their way!' He gave Boris's mother a tremendous hug. Then he came bounding across the room to Boris and hauled him out of bed.

'You're coming to town with me, my lad,' he boomed joyfully. 'I'm pretty sure there'll be food parcels for the children in the very first train.'

Boris looked at his mother. She was sitting right up in bed. It was as if this tremendous news had given her new life. Her face was quite different – she looked young and happy . . . just as she had before. Instead of being glazed with fever, her lovely brown eyes shone with joy.

'Oh, Vanya, is it really true?' she asked.

Boris gave a big sigh. The last clouds of uncertainty rolled away. It's really happened, he thought, the miracle really has happened . . .

That was a day that Boris would never forget. Even on the way to the station with Uncle Vanya it was evident that dying Leningrad was not going to die after all. Everyone seemed to be walking more erect, as if they had swallowed some magic potion that had given them new power. The German artillery had peppered the city with incendiary bombs. Now, as always, women were on the roofs. Risking their lives, they handed down the unexploded bombs with asbestos-gloved hands to other women who plunged them into tanks of water or snow. Now, as always, people were at work clearing the rubble and trying to bring some order to the chaotic streets. Now, as always, bodies lay in the snow, either killed in the night's raid or dying of sheer exhaustion.

But a new spirit of hope was running through the city. It was on all the faces, in all the excited voices that called from one side of the street to the other.

'It's the beginning of the end . . .'

'Now there'll be some food . . .'

'Reinforcements are on their way . . .'

'We're not on our own any longer . . .'

The first train steamed cheerfully in, and by noon a beginning had been made with the distribution of the food. Thanks to Uncle Vanya, Boris was near the front of the queue. One stamp on his ration card and the precious bundle was in his hands: tins of milk, and meat and chocolate. What happiness! Should he open the chocolate now, just to look? No, he would keep it until he got home and he and Mother would open everything together. Once again Boris walked along the streets of Leningrad. He thought about Nadia. If only the trains had got through a week earlier, perhaps the food parcels would have been in time to save Nadia's life . . . Then she might have become a film actress and made people laugh.

Boris began to feel sad again and to notice the ghostly

shells of the houses he was passing. For how many of the people who had lived in them had the food parcels arrived too late?

Suddenly his way was blocked. The paths among the snow were crowded with people. The women laying bricks had thrown down their tools and were clambering down from their trestles. A strange uneasiness blew through the street with the north wind. What was happening? On the other side a thick row of bystanders had formed. You couldn't believe so many could come so quickly, thought Boris. In the distance appeared a troop of soldiers. Were they men who had freed the railway? Was everyone going to cheer them for their courage? Hastily Boris got himself a place at the front. Behind him more and more people thronged.

'It's the Germans! The Germans!'

Suddenly everyone fell silent. A military truck lumbered past. In it stood men of the Red Army with machine-guns at the ready. And behind marched German prisoners-of-war in rows of four.

No one said a word. The only sounds were the shambling footsteps on the hard frozen snow.

Boris looked at the faces of the people around him. Drawn faces, fighting against emotions. One man opposite him watched with such unconcealed hatred in his eyes that Boris shivered. An old woman made the sign of the cross. An ambulance man bit his lips and swore under his breath.

The Germans! Still the deathly silence was unbroken. On they came, the murderers who had stabbed the city to its heart. In rows of four they marched past. Some still wore their helmets; others had green caps with ear flaps; some were bareheaded and kept their gloveless

hands in their sleeves. A few were wounded; they leaned on their comrades' shoulders, their faces twisted with pain.

The Germans! An endless trail of them tramped through the silence that said more than words; past the reproachful ruins; past the emptiness that had once held families they had destroyed; past men who had lost their wives, past widows, past orphans; past the dead still unburied in the snow.

The Germans! There they went with their shame and their guilt. Boris felt chilled to the heart; he too bit his lips, for it was a terrible sight: so many grown men, their courage vanished and their spirits broken, plodding on like beaten dogs. Here and there one of them would raise his head for an instant, then quickly lower it again. All around them lay silent, scarred Leningrad. No cry of distress from the ruins, no scream of a starving child, no curses of hate and anger could have hurt more deeply than that accusing silence.

The Germans! Boris had hated them for many months. But now they were trudging by, unshaven, dead-tired, out of step; now they had nothing left but their defeat and their guilt. Boris felt his throat tighten – this journey of retreat was so inhuman. He could have cried with shame at this moment of triumph. Where was any cause for joy now? He thought of his father, of Nadia, who had loved people so . . . With a shock Boris remembered the German officer; was he walking among these pitiful rows of spiritless, hopeless men?

Frantically Boris searched the German faces. Suddenly the face of one young soldier sprang to his sight. He had a bandage round his head, and his fair hair lifted in the cold wind. But it was the eyes under the bandage – Boris saw in them pain and confusion and despair and grief. The young soldier had his arms on the shoulders of two other Germans. They helped him over the icy street, through the degrading silence of the watching people.

Boris was overwhelmed with pity. Behind him he could feel the hate and bitterness of his fellow Russians; all around him were the ruins of the battered city. But suddenly he was convinced that something had to be done; that this was the time to show everyone that there were good Germans as well as bad.

It took a lot of courage to do what Boris did then, to defy the hundreds of people watching at the side of the road. But he did it. He sprang from the pavement and ran to the young wounded German. He pulled the bar of chocolate out of his bundle and pushed it into the soldier's hand. The row halted for a moment. The German's eyes lightened. Instead of a wounded, beaten, captive animal, he looked like a man again. He looked intently at Boris and smiled his thanks.

Then he was past. But Boris would never forget their meeting. With a profound sense of gratitude he stared after the Germans. It was almost impossible, but it was so; one small bar of chocolate had given a kind of firmness to their dragging feet. Slowly Boris went back to his place, his eyes on the ground. He didn't dare to look up, but he felt a hundred reproachful eyes looking at him, and on all sides he heard disapproving voices:

'They're devils – what did you do that for?'

'Do you call yourself a Russian?'

Then Boris felt someone lay a hand on his shoulder, and in a moment of silence an old woman's voice said, for everyone to hear: 'You did right, child.'

Boris looked up. The old woman was looking at him. Her wrinkled face was half-hidden by her black shawl, but her eyes were bright.

'You did right.' She turned to the people around them. 'What use is our freedom to us if we still live in hate?'

There was a pause, then most people nodded. Because those who have suffered much, can forgive much . . .

POSTSCRIPT

A thick layer of snow covered the Peskaryovskoye grave-yard, where the victims of the war had been laid to rest in a mass grave. Almost 700,000 men, women and children perished during the siege of Leningrad, which lasted for 900 days altogether. It was December 1965. The frost was bitter and an icy wind blew incessantly over the white graves, but Boris did not seem to feel the cold.

'Whenever I feel at odds with myself, with God, with people, with the world, I always come back to this place,' he said shyly, as if a grown man should not make such a confession.

Towering over the graves was a great monument, in front of it an eternal flame; it seemed to say that the souls of the dead had brought warmth to the living by giving their lives for them. Boris read out the words that had been engraved on the sombre granite:

> Here lie the citizens of Leningrad.
> Here lie our comrades – men, women and children.
> Beside them lie the men of the Red Army.
> With their lives they defended you, beloved Lenin-
>   grad.
> Too many to number
> Are the glorious names of those
> Who are buried beneath this everlasting marble.
> Stranger, who stand beside these stones, know
> That no one is forgotten
> That nothing is forgotten . . .

There was a silence. Boris hunched deeper into his coat.

'I survived the war all right,' he went on. 'During the siege 5,000 high explosives and 100,000 incendiaries fell, and the city was under gunfire 150,000 times. Five million square metres of our land were devastated or badly damaged. Scarcely a house remained intact.' He smiled again, rather ruefully . . . 'Yes, I survived the war all right, but sometimes I found it difficult to accept so-called peace and freedom. Nadia was right when she wrote in her diary: 'Freedom only comes when everyone is happy.' His gaze wandered over to the snow-covered graves as if he sought the place where Nadia was buried.

'Nadia did appear in a film after all,' said Boris, and he nodded towards the flame. 'After the war they made a documentary film called *The Siege of Leningrad*, and it opened with her picture and some lines from her diary. She never made people laugh, as she so much wanted to do, but she made them cry and really touched their hearts. That's more than one can say of most film stars.' Boris shrugged his shoulders and looked a little less sad.

'After the war I did all sorts of things, but I couldn't settle down. I was always a rebel. I worked with my hands; I studied; but I couldn't ever find a purpose to life. I had grown too old to remember how wise a child can be. Nadia loved people. She had found the answer and it was the right answer . . .'

He stared into the distance, where the church spires pointed to heaven with the patience of centuries.

'At last I took up writing,' continued Boris. 'And as I grew older I began to grope little by little towards the answer, which Nadia and I, as children, had already known so well. I married and now I have two children

who, thank God, have never known what war is.' Then
he waved a hand over the graves for the last time. 'And
here they lie, who made it all possible . . .'

It was icy cold, but I was warmed by the eternal flame.
I was glad that Boris had brought me there.